Creative Giving

Hiley H. Ward

The Macmillan Company
New York
1958

First Printing

Library of Congress catalog card number: 58-12072

The Macmillan Company, New York
Brett-Macmillan Ltd., Galt, Ontario

Printed in the United States of America

To
CHARLOTTE

Partner in Giving

Acknowledgments

With gratitude, the author wishes to acknowledge his indebtedness to T. K. Thompson, executive director of the Joint Department of Stewardship and Benevolence, National Council of Churches, who gave his wholehearted assistance by providing books and source materials and by reading and offering critical suggestions on the working synopsis and the final draft; to Harl Russell, Church of the Brethren, for his assistance in the early stages of the book and as consultant on stewardship questions; to stewardship leaders in Chicago, Minneapolis, New York City, Washington, and Nashville, who gave their time so generously in personal interviews; to more than one hundred others who lent their assistance in the United States and around the world; to the library staffs of Catholic University of America, Jewish Theological Seminary, Library of Congress, McCormick Theological Seminary, Garrett Biblical Institute, Gail Borden Library, Elgin, Illinois: and to Mrs. Byron Bey, who typed the manuscript.

Helping to mold a rough draft into final shape were the suggestions and opinions of readers to whom the author owes special thanks. Reading the entire manuscript were Mrs. Iva S. Hoth, Dundee, Illinois; Dr. T. A. Kantonen, professor of systematic theology, Hamma Divinity School, Springfield, Ohio; Dr. Guy H. Ranson, professor of Christian ethics, The Southern Baptist Theological Seminary, Louisville, Kentucky. Reading the Old Testament sections was Dr. Douglas C. Stephens, associate professor of Old Testament, Northern Baptist Seminary, Chicago; reading the New Testament sections was Dr. Floyd V. Filson, professor of New Testament literature and history, McCormick Theological Seminary, Chicago. The views of readers and advisers are not necessarily represented by the book.

Contents

1

What Is Creative Giving?

Soldiers, mingling with the wide-eyed crowd at the execution that had been going on for three hours on Skull's hill outside Jerusalem, were impervious to the groans and cries of anguish that came down from the crosses, but there were those there who felt in their souls each moment of agony. They knew what it was to suffer; they were an oppressed people in an occupied land. They believed in justice, which was one reason they had trudged up the hill to the execution: The subjects on the crosses all deserved to die—both the thieves who did not hesitate to cut throats to take bread earned by the sweat of another's hands and the forlorn figure from Herod's territory who was foolish enough to say that he was the Son of God. That is why the people laughed—that is why the multitude on Golgotha's crown wagged their heads at him and shouted with laughter: for how could anyone be so foolish as to think he was the Son of God in a land where rebellion was a disease punishable by the dreadful suffering of crucifixion. The people laughed at the sign in Latin, in the vernacular, and in the holy language of the Hebrews—"Jesus of Nazareth, King of the Jews."

As the soldiers began to toss their dice, the crowds continued to laugh and mock.

But a profound feeling must have begun to grow on certain onlookers that day. Who had ever thought of the Son of God being crucified with thieves? Some from both the elite of Israel and the peasantry—Nicodemus, Joseph of Arimathea, the women beneath the cross—surely discerned in a small way that the weakness of man was the strength of God. Could the learned men of the Temple, now that the deed was done, escape entirely the familiar words of Isaiah?—"He is despised and rejected of men; a man of sorrows, and acquainted with grief: and we hid as it were our faces from him; he was despised, and we esteemed him not."[1] When it was all over one soldier looked up and exclaimed, "Truly this man was a son of God!"[2]

This awakening thought must have brought a chill to the minds of some of these spectators, revealing to them that this unexpected turn of events was a divine novelty, the work of the creative hand of God.

The events of God are never really fully understood; the more men have tried to ponder them, the more they have raised clouds of confusion and error. It was the so-called men of God who erred the most that day, for they crucified the flesh of God himself. Men can never really understand nor anticipate the acts of God. That is the novelty of God. When God acts, his deeds appear new to man, though they are timeless, neither old nor new with God. Christ was "slain from the foundation of the world,"[3] but his death appears new and is new today to each one who submits to the cleansing power of the cross. The acts of a creative and a redemptive God appear as acts of novelty. Even as Jesus' followers were still pondering the swift events of the previous week and the cataclysmic crucifixion, they were to experience an act without parallel in history—one which they could not comprehend nor anticipate, although they were forewarned. For those who brought spices for the dead, the tomb had a startling revelation. It was empty. It was unbelievable to Thomas: "Except I shall see in his hands the prints of the nails . . ." Thomas said, "I will not believe."[4]

[1] Isaiah 53: 3.
[2] Mark 15: 39 (RSV).
[3] Revelation 13: 8.
[4] John 20: 25.

The resurrection is entirely novel. It is the pivotal event of Christianity—the one which distinguishes it from all other faiths.

Novelty is the essence of creativity in religion—particularly in Christianity. "You must be born anew,"[5] said Jesus.

Failure to pay attention to the newness in religion is always the demise of the contemporary religion. The Goths sacked Rome, the Reformation shook and splintered the medieval church, and the modern revival of non-Christian religions is crashing like a giant wrecking stone against the structure of Western Christianity. Unless there is a revived sense of newness instead of conformity, the disintegration of contemporary institutionalized Western religion can occur very rapidly.

The priority of novelty is always a hard lesson for conformity. The sudden launching of Russian satellites shocked the Western world. Such a thing could not happen. But it did. The sense of novelty in the West in regard to interplanetary science was becoming dull. But the sense of novelty took the initiative. Western propaganda and influence lost out to that which was the most novel. It is possible that the jolt came early enough, and not too late as it did in Rome, but the tragic thing about the sudden exposure of the West to novelty is that it represents such a small fragment of a person's experience—technological, physical sciences—and not the core of life itself. In other words, the most important part of a nation's life—its religious life—has not yet been exposed to the novelty of the spirit, and it is for this reason that the great cloud of doom hangs over Western civilization. It is not enough to try to match satellites in the heavens with greater and more far-reaching satellites. There must be novelty of the spirit.

Alarming are remarks such as those made by Dr. Rajah B. Manikam, head of the Tamil Evangelical Lutheran church of India, quoted recently in the public press. He said: "The belief that religion is an opiate of the people is gaining ground, especially among the student classes and workers in industries." Particularly, he says, this is true on the newer frontiers, such as Asia and Africa where

[5] John 3: 7 (RSV).

Buddhism and Mohammedanism are being revived with great success. Whether Christians are losing the battle in the contemporary scene, of course, cannot be judged historically. But remarks of such contemporary observers as Dr. Manikam and also Harry H. McLeod, of Forth Worth, Texas, who points out in the *Baptist Standard* that "the churches now influence society in inverse proportion to their numbers,"[6] sum up a popular opinion that the battle is not going so well. Novelty in religion is a subject that cannot be overlooked by conscientious Christians.

The whole relationship of God to man is novel. He formed (*barah*) or created the world—not *ex nihilo,* but the world as void and meaningless extension. God brought new shape, new purpose, life to the void. The novelty and creativity of God's actions are synonymous. The relationship of the Godhead to man through the person of Jesus Christ was certainly novel in the sense of the crucifixion and the resurrection. The coming of the Holy Spirit was novel in the way it came, in the way it works, and in what it accomplishes. "The spirit blows where it wishes,"[7] Jesus said. The relationship of God to man is one of creativity with novelty as a basic indication of that activity. And the life of the Christian in all of his relationships is creativity as seen in novelty, as one who is "born" anew. We are to "serve in newness of spirit."[8]

God's relationship to man can be further amplified in another word: Giving. "God so loved . . . he gave." This is the gospel within the gospel. The gift of God's son is good news, the divine novelty for every age, especially when creativity goes begging in religion and when institutionalized Christianity suffers from a lack of new life and purpose.

God gives. His creative action and novelty have always been illustrated by his giving. Prior to the Fall, man is in the Garden with everything at his disposal. When man misuses God's gift, he is cast out of the Garden. God recognizes Noah's righteousness and gives

[6] Harry H. McLeod, "What Is the Trend?" *Baptist Standard* (Texas: Southern Baptist, weekly), Sept. 7, 1957, p. 8.
[7] John 3: 8 (Greek—"*to pneuma hopou thelei pnei*").
[8] Romans 7: 6.

to him and his family a new world; to Abraham and Sarah in their old age he gives a son to be the father of his people; to the children of Israel in bondage he gives a Promised Land; he gives them the Ten Commandments.

Mixed, however, with God's merciful love and giving in the Old Testament are his justice and judgment. Thus while he metes out mercy and watches over the needs of his children, he is opposed to the power of sin and judges it, condemning and righting the wrong. When the children of Israel sin, they fall out of harmony with their giver. God's gifts become unwelcome. The Land which God promised seems too difficult to find, and the people prefer not to try.[9] The Israelites, who want the law, change their minds while Moses is on the Mount and build a golden calf. God becomes wrathful and punishment prevails; when Israel and Judah sin against God, they fall and disintegrate before their enemies. Thus God's demand for righteousness—his judgment upon the sinner and the wicked—is mixed with his mercy. But even when judgment exists, a gift of God always prevails and abounds. Thus Ezekiel in the midst of immediate dismay at the time of the Fall of Jerusalem foresees a better day. "And I the Lord will be their God . . ." Ezekiel reports. "And I will make them and the places round about my hill a blessing; and I will cause the shower to come down in his season; there shall be showers of blessing."[10] Giving, therefore, in the sense of loving-kindness and mercy, does not always stand out in the Old Testament. But when the whole picture of the relationship of an all-loving God to his creation is seen, giving is dominant. Giving, as depicting God's action toward men, is acute in the Old Testament, as it is under the grace of the new covenant; giving becomes an adequate description of the action and responsibility of God toward his creation.

Giving characterizes man's relationship to God, and man to man. "Give to him that asketh thee,"[11] Jesus says. "Freely ye have received,

[9] Numbers 14: 2, 3.
[10] Ezekiel 34: 24a, 26.
[11] Matthew 5: 42.

freely give."[12] "Give to the poor."[13] "Give, and it shall be given unto you."[14] Giving is activity. In Christianity, giving is responsible activity, a natural correlative of a God who gives. Everything Jesus said in a theological sense carries overtones of giving. "Give us this day our daily bread;"[15] "Come . . . and I will give you rest;"[16] "I will give unto thee the keys of the kingdom of heaven;"[17] Jesus gives thanks and praise to God.[18] "This is my body which is given for you;"[19] "The bread that I will give is my flesh, which I will give for the life of the world."[20] Preparing to give his own life as a ransom for many,[21] Jesus asks that his followers take up their cross and follow him.[22] The nature of the Christian gospel cries for it to be "given"—both in sharing the content of the good news (evangelism) and in responsible living.

Responsible living or action is often characterized by "stewardship." According to a report on stewardship at the Lutheran World Federation meeting in Minneapolis in 1957, stewardship includes both the "telling" and the "doing" of the gospel, although the report adequately recognizes the popular distinction in emphases, between evangelism and stewardship. As we continue, however, this author prefers to avoid the word "stewardship" in defining "responsible action" for these reasons as well as the philological reasons on page 132.

1. Stewardship is not a convincing Biblical word—appearing only about eighteen times in the King James as compared to the nearly one thousand uses of "giving" in terms of man's relationship both to his fellowman and to God. Stewardship tends to be no more than a vocational usage in such verses as Matthew 20: 8

[12] Matthew 10: 8.
[13] Matthew 19: 21.
[14] Luke 6: 38.
[15] Matthew 6: 11.
[16] Matthew 11: 28.
[17] Matthew 16: 19.
[18] Matthew 21: 16; Mark 8: 6; John 11: 41.
[19] Luke 22: 19.
[20] John 6: 51.
[21] Mark 10: 45.
[22] Mark 8: 34.

("The Lord of the vineyard saith unto his steward, Call the labourers . . .") and Luke 8: 3 ("the wife of Chuza Herod's steward"). The vocation could have been that of centurion or publican as well as that of steward.

2. The Hebrew and Greek forms for stewardship vary considerably in meanings. For example, in the Old Testament these Hebrew phrases are all translated "steward"—"The man who is over" *(ha-'ish 'asher 'al,* Genesis 43: 19); "who is over a house" *('asher 'al bayith,* Genesis 44: 4); "Son of acquisition" (*ben mesheg,* Genesis 15: 2); "prince, head, chief, captain" (*sar,* 1 Chronicles 28: 1). In the New Testament, there are two basic words that are translated "steward"—"One to whom a thing is committed" (*epitropos*) and "a house manager" (*oikonomos,* with the variations *oikonomeo,* "to be a house manager," and *oikonomia,* "house management" or "stewardship"). The two basic Greek words are not always translated "steward."[23]

3. The Christian's relationship to God and his Savior is more than that of "house manager." The wells of spiritual relationship are rooted in active communion and not in management (John 15).

4. Since both *epitropos* and *oikonomos* carry connotations of something which is left behind, a more active expression might be more descriptive of the Christian life, for example, such a denotation of *oikonomos* as "commission."

5. Stewardship is not uniquely theistic—it is well at home in deism when God is in his heaven and all is believed to be well on earth.

6. The idea of stewardship in its familiar usage limits the respon-

[23] For example, when they appear together in Galatians 4: 2 they are rendered in the King James "tutors" (*epitropous*) and "governors" (*oikonomous*). *Epitropos* means literally "control of anything left behind," thus a "bailiff, agent, manager;" *oikonomos,* the more common of the New Testament words for "steward," means literally "house manager," but it takes on deeper spiritual significance than the literal meaning in such passages as 1 Peter 4: 10 where, according to Harper's *Analytical Greek Lexicon,* it can mean "the holder of a commission" (Goodspeed translates "dispersers") or in 1 Timothy 1: 4 (oikonomia), "a due discharge of a commission" (ASV translates "dispensation") which seems to be a more adequate translation than the King James "edifying" (RSV—"training") or the literal idea of "house management" or "vocational (in a spiritual sense) stewardship."

sibility of the Christian. It is one-directional—God the owner and man the steward. It does not generally include any recognition of the responsible relationship between man and man. With Jesus both areas of responsibility were important.[24] So as we continue, we shall speak of responsibility in terms of giving, not stewardship.

"Giving" pinpoints better than any other word God's action and man's responsibility—that is, the responsibility of the man who is "born again," in whom the Spirit moves and has full course. Such a person who receives the free, unreserved gift of God becomes a giving creature. He is radiant—as a bulb on a giant yuletide tree at nighttime. The community knows he is different. And in him is the potentiality of changing the world. He lives. He gives. ". . . I live; yet not I, but Christ liveth in me: and . . . I live by the faith of the Son of God, who . . . gave himself for me."[25] He is an agent of grace, making the *kerygma* or message of Jesus available to every creature—in word and deed.

The Christian should be conscious of his giving relationship. In Jesus' parable of the unforgiving servant,[26] the servant expected his Lord to forgive him of a great debt. But the servant in turn would not forgive his fellow servant who owed him a much smaller sum. The unforgiving servant had a responsibility which he did not recognize. He failed to give or forgive, even though his Lord had given him his pardon. The Christian is not to be like the unforgiving servant, for the Christian is expected to give in every sense of the word. Psychologically, he will be willing to forgive the grudges and weaknesses of others, as his master was willing to forgive him of his sins; sociologically, he will work for the realization of the Kingdom of God, employing his time, intelligence, resources; he will give spiritually—in worship to God, in propagating the gospel among his fellow men, and in his use of special gifts enjoined by the Spirit; he will give aesthetically by whatever talents or genius God has endowed him with, and so on. In whatsoever he does he will give.

[24] Matthew 22: 37-40.
[25] Galatians 2: 20.
[26] Matthew 18: 23-35.

What will it actually cost him to give? We know what it means when a creative God gives and what it costs him. We know, too, that following Jesus is a costly as well as a new and creative venture. "And whosoever doth not bear his cross, and come after me, cannot be my disciple. For which of you, intending to build a tower, sitteth not down first, and counteth the cost, whether he have sufficient to finish it?"[27]

The cost is great. That is a matter that each person must face as he answers Jesus' call and enters a new state. The cost must be considered ahead of time, for a condition of the Kingdom is that it is not to be dependent on the things past or future. There is no looking back, nor a second look.[28]

Jesus expects his followers to live, and to give, creatively.

Before we enter a discussion of traditional giving and examine the roots of modern giving in relationship to creative religion, it is necessary to see what creative giving is.

Creative giving may be described by three illustrations.

I

As a father comes home from a day's work, he is glad to see his youngsters run to him, throw their arms around him, or in some way express their gratitude at seeing him. The questions which sometimes come, however, may be disturbing, such as, "What did you bring me, Daddy?"

Now you and I teach our children not to ask such a question. Nevertheless the busy adult has to face this question occasionally whether the child expresses it or not. The substance of the question can be put in a statement, as in the mind of the father: "I should like to give something to Jane and Mike now."

Now the father has two courses of action if he is to fulfill his immediate wish.

1. If he has not brought a surprise ahead of time, he can go to the neighborhood store and bring back a surprise; or even for that matter

[27] Luke 14: 27, 28.
[28] Luke 9: 62.

he can take the children with him, give them a nickel or two apiece, and let them pick out the items of their choice; the enthusiasm and the expression on their faces will be reward enough for the father.

2. Not having prepared a gift, he could pull out objects of interest from his coat to give to the children, such as gum, a tag, pin, an old key. Or he could dispense with material gifts and say, "I didn't bring a toy; I brought a kiss."

Consider the results of the two types of giving. In the deliberative act, a thought of reward—expectancy—cannot be separated from the act itself, thus bringing in self-interest; in the second act the result may be negative—the child might prefer a material object in the place of the kiss, depending largely on the age of the child. But if there is a clear distinction between the two types of gifts offered, which is hypothetical in this case, the affectionate father will probably serve the interests of the child in the long run by not giving a gift bound by routine or expectancy, although as a sincere giver he may not at the outset be appreciated.

This presents two aspects of creative giving—the *motive* and the *result*. Motive, devoid of any subtle expectancy of reward, will be altruistic, not concerned with self-interest, and the result of the creative act may fail to bring appreciation or recognition. This was Jesus' experience—he had a task to accomplish, a life to give. He did not have to die on a cross for his own sake. He is a part of the Godhead prior to the Incarnation, and he could have called down legions to prevent his sacrifice on the cross; certainly he was assured of a place at the right hand of God with powers of judgment,[29] mediation,[30] and authority.[31] He clearly gave no thought to the reward—this being impossible since he was "very God of very God" himself. In his action, devoid of a mundane desire for reward, his motive is clear. It was love.

We cannot dwell for any length on the word "love," for, being the essence of God's revelation, like God, love is literally meaningless when forced into the limitations of definition. Ever try to explain

[29] Hebrews 10: 12, 13.
[30] Hebrews 9: 15.
[31] Romans 1: 4.

who God is? We know that this cannot be done without becoming entangled in the relevancy of the terms of language. For example, we say that God is good; but that does not define God either, for "good" is also an abstraction, as are the terms "God" and "love." If we try to be more specific, and actually say that "the man up there" has Gregory Peck's eyes, Jeff Chandler's gray, wavy hair, then we have reached the absurd, of course, and are defining God purely in terms of man, as the ancients did their gods. The truth is that nothing concrete or literally meaningful can be said directly about God. Two early church thinkers (the man who wrote under the pseudonym of Dionysius the Areopagite in the fifth century and John Scotus Erigena who wrote in the ninth) emphasized this approach. Thus they talked of the negative way (*via negativa*). They could either describe what God is *not* or what he is *like*. But never what he is. This is true in regard to love. We can only talk of what it is like—and this is the way Jesus talked of it, for example, when he said "Greater love hath no man than this, that a man lay down his life for his friends."[32] Other religions talk of love; some segments of Christianity try to approach it definitively. Some even idolize it. All that Jesus could do was to illustrate it.

The "charity" or "love" (RSV) chapter (1 Corinthians 13) tells us what love is not and what it is like. It is not—

· proud
· faith or confidence by itself
· only feeding the poor
· martyrdom
· envious
· rash
· puffed up
· misbehaving
· self-seeking
· easily irritated
· evil-minded
· happy with evil or misfortune.

[32] John 15: 13.

The same chapter tells us what love is like. It is like a person who—

- suffers long
- is kind
- rejoices in the truth
- bears all things
- believes all things
- hopes all things
- endures all things.

Never can we say with a word exactly what love is, for any other virtue, such as faith or hope, is inferior to it. Love is the greatest of all. We have to be content merely with saying what it is not or what it is like. That is also the danger of defining love. While groping for a definition and trying to lay hold of it, it escapes us. The more Christianity reaches for a definition of love, the more it eludes the pursuers, as the "weightier matters of the law"[33] eluded the pernicious efforts of the Pharisees. Actually, the closest we can come to the meaning of love is in action, even as God did by approaching it in crucifixion. Creative giving brings us closest to the meaning of love.

If God is love[34] and if God is a giving God,[35] then love and giving are coextensive. God who gives also loves, and although the difference between the two attributes is not apprehended by man's logic, the correlation of the two is obvious in the atoning work of Christ. "To give and to keep on giving is the essential nature of God who is love," says Professor T. A. Kantonen of Hamma (United Lutheran) Divinity School, Springfield, Ohio. "Christian giving thus mirrors faithfully the nature of God and the nature of Christian stewardship."[36]

Love does not exist for a person's own satisfaction. Nicolas Berdyaev, who fled Russian Communism, points out that "all creativ-

[33] Matthew 23: 23.
[34] 1 John 4: 8.
[35] John 3: 16; Romans 8: 32.
[36] T. A. Kantonen, *A Theology for Christian Stewardship* (Philadelphia: Muhlenberg Press, 1956), p. 42.

ity . . . is love. . . . If you wish to receive, give; if you wish to feel satisfaction, do not seek it, never think of it, yea, forget the very word."[37] Love, too, as a means to satisfaction, must be forgotten. In the gesture of Berdyaev, let us also forget the word, and seek its meaning in creative activity.

Creative giving, then, has as its motive *love*—both an indefinable and a relevant term—and as we have noted in passing, the result of creative giving, may not be appreciated in human society, even as God's "unspeakable gift"[38] lacks any great degree of appreciation.

II

When we enter church on Sunday, we are confronted with opportunities to give. We can bring our gifts in two manners: (1) Giving the percentage that one plans from week to week, or (2) we can make an "offering." While the gift as an offering may be planned, it is distinguished from percentage or proportionate giving where the amount remains the same for a general period of time and where it is determined in ratio to a whole. The second way of giving, by means of an offering or a response, is creative giving.

Both the Old and New Testaments are built upon giving in the sense of offerings—both covenants are sealed by covenant offerings involving the shedding of blood—in the Old Testament the sacrificing of animals, in the New the shedding of the blood of the lamb without blemish, Jesus Christ. Cain and Abel brought their offerings. When Moses gathered the people together to direct them in the building of the tabernacle, he told them that God commanded each man to take a part in bringing gifts that would help to construct the tabernacle. He told them what was needed: "Take ye from among you an offering unto the Lord: whosoever is of a willing heart, let him bring it, an offering of the Lord; gold, and silver, and brass. . . ."[39] This offering did not involve calculation or sameness in

[37] *The Destiny of Man* (New York: Charles Scribner's Sons, 1937), p. 181.
[38] 2 Corinthians 9: 15.
[39] Exodus 35: 5.

giving. "And they came, every one whose heart stirred him up, and every one whom his spirit made willing, and they brought the Lord's offering to the work of the tabernacle. . . . And they came, both men and women, as many as were willing hearted. . . ."[40] They gave as a response, as their hearts were stirred.

Giving, when it is creative, is a *response*. Creativity in industry often comes as the result of communion with industry's most vital source—the body of consumers, their remarks, the research conclusions. Likewise, creativity for the Christian and the church is the result of communion with the source—God, through his Son, Jesus Christ. When giving is creative, acting in response, it escapes the realm of ethical decision and the qualms of conscience. Dietrich Bonhoeffer, who was hanged by the Nazis because his response to God took the form of concrete action against Hitler, said: "The man who acts ideologically sees himself justified in his idea; the responsible man commits his action into the hands of God and lives by God's grace and favour."[41]

Living in response to God permits a man to assert his *freedom*—both the freedom and independence of his nature and the new freedom which he has in Christ. Man is born to be free. This is especially true of the Christian, whose new birth frees him from the bondage of sin and the old habits. "The truth shall make you free."[42] Disciplines can help to guide the Christian, to correct him, to remind him when he is tempted to enter the old ways. But his action will be in the sphere of freedom where he makes his decisions day by day, moment by moment in response to Christ.

Creative giving, emerging out of an awareness of freedom in the new life, is characterized by *immediacy*. Christ is here. There is a sense of urgency—the immediacy which characterizes Christian evangelism also applies to Christian giving in regard to one's pos-

[40] Exodus 35: 21, 22.

[41] Dietrich Bonhoeffer, *Ethics* (New York: The Macmillan Company, 1955), p. 204. On the same page Bonhoeffer explains responsible (historical) action: "Ultimate ignorance of one's own good and evil, and with it a complete reliance upon grace, is an essential property of responsible historical action."

[42] John 8: 32.

sessions and interests. "Now is the day of salvation"[43] can also mean for Christians that now, as "good stewards (or holders of a commission) of the manifold grace of God,"[44] is the time for Christians to give.

Several weeks prior to this writing, I stood alone one night beneath the Washington monument, gazing first at the lights of the city, then peering up at the huge shaft that so silently blended with the sky. Nothing else seemed to exist except the great monument which appeared out of place in a busy city. So it is with the cross and its crucified subject. The crucified Christ towers over every decision of the Christian. We are new creatures and abide every moment with Christ. "Abide in me, and I in you . . . continue ye in my love."[45]

When Paul asked the Christians at Corinth to prepare a gift for the Jerusalem church, he had one request: "I should like it to be a spontaneous gift, and not money squeezed out of you by what I have said."[46]

When giving is from the heart, it is characterized by *spontaneity*, and in its perpetual newness it is always creative.

III

A city's streets provide opportunities for giving—to the alcoholic who asks for a dime for a cup of coffee, to solicitors who appeal for children's funds, for cancer or heart research, for veterans' aid or for muscular dystrophy.

Several years ago, a friend and I were taking photographs for an article about Chicago's skid row. A shabby man leaning on a cane amidst bleak surroundings with a gaudy whisky sign as background made a striking subject. One of the Chicago newspapers, conducting a crusade to clean up skid row, had created an antagonism among the men of the row which we were quick to discover. As we snapped the picture, the man suddenly raised the cane and a hand in protest.

[43] 2 Corinthians 6: 2.
[44] 1 Peter 4: 10.
[45] John 15: 4, 9.
[46] 2 Corinthians 9: 5 (Phillips, *Letters to Young Churches*).

When the picture was developed, he did not look as if he were about to strike, but rather as if he were begging for alms.

A picture of such a man is a symbol of the outcasts of the streets. His hand raised as if to beg alms, he resents everything connected with life—its institutions, its customs, the concrete on which he makes his bed night after night. His resentment becomes mixed with his alms asking, as revealed in our picture. Most Christians are thankful that they have little contact with such a person. Yet this man is one for whom Christ died—a man on whom there is a premium in the Kingdom of God, since Christ came to save sinners and not merely to call the righteous to repentance.[47]

Toyohiko Kagawa, a dynamic little man of Japan, was troubled by the depravity on the streets of Tokyo. Beggars and derelicts were everywhere, dirty, sick, hungry. Being a Christian, Kagawa wanted to help. What could he do? Consider his alternatives: (1) giving money to a beggar or needy person, or (2) taking the person home, giving of his own substance, time, interests, love (expressed by the things nearest to him or that meant the most to him, such as the companionship of the family, the fire on the hearth, the food on the table, the joy of a hobby or recreation).

The second was Kagawa's choice. As a Christian he could not confine his giving to institutions or to anonymous figures on the street. He had to become personally involved, as the Good Samaritan who took the wounded Jew to an inn and assured him of housing, food, and medicine to lead him on the road to recovery. The task was especially great for Kagawa. Coming from a well-to-do background in which he had become sole heir to his father's estate, he was accustomed to fine things. On becoming a Christian, he was disinherited. But this did not put a check on his giving potential. Penniless, he makes his way in a greatly overcrowded population by cleaning chimneys. This enables him to buy his meals of rice soup each day. But this was not enough—he went into "the streets and lanes of the city"[48] and rounded up the sick, the beggars, and even

[47] Mark 2: 17.
[48] Luke 14: 21.

a murderer and invited them home to share a bowl of diluted soup. Never did he escape an "I-Thou" (*ich-du*)[49] relationship with God or his fellow men. He saw each man as a person, as Christ sees him. Giving, as he practices it, is *personal.*

Kagawa's giving is also *total*—it embraces the whole self. Kagawa was not content merely to visit prisoners, the underprivileged, the sick, the dying, the neglected, on Sunday afternoons. He lived with his giving. Every moment was part of the whole—a series of indivisible moments, a life in time dedicated to the risen Savior. He could not escape his obligation to give continually in a total way.

The Jews were taught to think in terms of totality—the Shema states that the Lord our God is one Lord and that the Jews were to be conscious of God's word when sitting in their houses or when walking or lying down.[50] Jesus expresses the same feeling. He repeats the great commandment of Deuteronomy 6: 5 and adds Leviticus 19: 18. Said Jesus to the lawyer: "Thou shalt love the Lord thy God with all thy heart, and with all thy soul, and with all thy mind, and with all thy strength . . . and the second is like, namely this, Thou shalt love thy neighbour as thyself."[51]

When the Jewish literalists tried to confound Jesus with a question about giving, Jesus spoke in such terms of totality of giving that his interrogators were thrown into complete confusion. Their laws and customs had taught them to think in terms of proportion, of divided spheres in living. Thus their question: "Is it lawful to give tribute unto Caesar, or not?" Jesus' answer: "Show me the tribute money. . . . Whose is this image and superscription?" If he answered, "Caesar's," the people would be angry; if he said "God's," the Romans would have cause to hold him in account. Jesus answered: "Render therefore unto Caesar the things which are Caesar's; and unto God the things that are God's."[52]

[49] An idea that God and people are related as persons (and not as objects) made popular by the German-Jewish philosopher Martin Buber, with the publication of his *Ich und Du* in 1923 and its English translation in 1937.
[50] Deuteronomy 6: 7.
[51] Mark 12: 30, 31.
[52] Matthew 22: 15-22.

Giving, Jesus says, is more than a money concept. It involves the person, the total arena of existence. A man can give one coin both to God and to Caesar at the same time—but in his giving, whether it be to Caesar, a manufacturer, the church—he is to be conscious of his responsibility, making sure by many means that he is acting responsibly. When paying taxes to a government, he can follow through with prayer, exercising his franchise, witnessing for what he believes. Thus he serves God and Caesar. In purchasing, as well as in church contributions, he should be sure that his act will give the maximum amount of glory possible to God. It is a total task, a total responsibility that the "new" man faces.

Obviously all coins could not go directly to Caesar. Some money Jesus permitted to be kept for the daily needs of his little band,[53] some money he paid to Caesar. Jesus purposely avoids a division of monies. He knew the frailty and limitations of human terminology, which could be twisted to mean many things; in addition, he thought in terms of the total life—total commitment and the total response.

The creative giver, who is totally involved, goes out in sympathy to every subject or person he meets. He is *empathic,* suffering with the needy, not copying the sufferer, but bearing with him. "He comes into the presence of God," as Howard Thurman says, "with the smell of life about him."[54]

A Russian youth, asked by an American why he did not buy shoes for his torn feet, explained: "I cannot afford to buy myself shoes, when there are millions who have never heard about Communism." He felt linked to the needs of his fellow men. Christians, being inextricably linked with their fellow men, are also on a creative venture, not shrouded in Communistic pessimism, but enveloped by a living presence. "Rejoice," says Peter, "inasmuch as ye are partakers of Christ's sufferings; that when his glory shall be revealed, ye may be glad also with exceeding joy. . . .

[53] John 13: 29.

[54] Howard Thurman, *The Creative Encounter* (New York: Harper and Brothers, 1954), p. 23.

"Wherefore let them that suffer according to the will of God commit the keeping of their souls to him in well doing, as unto a faithful Creator."[55] This, then, is creative giving for the Christian—a commitment to God and a sharing in the sufferings of Christ, who died on the behalf of man. Of course, we cannot share his vicarious responsibility, but we can bear our responsibility and share the sorrows of others, pointing them to Jesus who is the "Shepherd and Bishop" of our souls[56] and who invited those that "labour and are heavy laden" to come unto him.[57]

A Christian who is a partaker of Christ's suffering is a creative giver. Every situation has a freshness and newness about it. He has *love*, a state of existence rather than a motive per se, as his theme, not seeking a reward. He acts out of *response* characterized by *freedom, immediacy, spontaneity*. The scope of his action is *personal, total, empathic*. Yet if one word were to be selected from all of these, it would be "spontaneity." For it is in spontaneity that God, through the complete novelty of his own Son on a cross in this world, meets man, and it is the way his creatures, experiencing a new life in Christ, are impelled to give.

Spontaneity is the giving most consistent with the unrestricted and unprompted action of the Spirit. But before we examine spontaneity more fully, let us look at contemporary giving as characterized by proportionate giving. Then we shall look more closely at spontaneity, face some of its problems head on, and see if Christians who remain constantly under temptation can be expected to give in this ideal way.

[55] 1 Peter 4: 13, 19.
[56] 1 Peter 2: 25.
[57] Matthew 11: 28.

2

What's Wrong with Proportionate Giving?

Practical-minded Western churches speak of a proportion as a starting point for giving and of "time, abilities, and possessions" as the categories of giving.

Most churches in the United States and Canada subscribe to a common creed of giving. Originated by the National Council of Churches of Christ in the United States of America, the statement is accepted officially by such groups as the Baptist Federation of Canada and the Church of God in the United States which belong to the Department of Stewardship and Benevolence of the National Council, although they do not belong as denominations to the Council. The statement is: "Christian Stewardship is the practice of systematic and proportionate giving of time, abilities, and material possessions based on the conviction that these are a trust from God, to be used in His service for the benefit of all mankind in grateful acknowledgement of Christ's redeeming love."

How does a person give proportionately? Following are two popular ideas of proportionate giving, a maximum and a minimum:

1. The *Memphis Press-Scimitar* carried an interview recently with a Christian businessman whose thirty-million-dollar industry gives 90 per cent of its stock to an endowment fund to aid churches

and other religious enterprises. The giving of ninety dollars out of one hundred is proportionate giving. Said the headline of the article: "It's all the Lord's money: only tenth for himself." There is 10 per cent, which at least as the newspaper interpreted it, is marked "hands off" to God.

2. At the other end of the scale another Christian millionaire from Texas made the headlines in 1957 by giving a tithe, or one-tenth, of his net capital to his church. After signing papers turning the stock of his oil company over to another firm, he reportedly received thirty-five million dollars. With taxes deducted, there remained about twenty million, and from this came the tithe of two million.

It is this latter idea of giving 10 per cent that has become the fad of twentieth century Protestant giving.

From where did the idea of tithing come?

How and why has tithing gained popularity? (The following chart indicates the widespread popularity of tithing, its late appearance on the modern scene, and its predominance as an American practice.)

Is there anything wrong with tithing?

To discuss creative giving, one must first look at the current trend, tithing. To understand tithing will be to meet some of the subtle problems of Western giving and to see current giving in the perspective of creative religion.

Let us look into (1) the history of tithing, (2) the influence of the historical pattern of tithing on Protestant, Roman Catholic, and Jewish attitudes today, (3) the pressures or currents which have brought a new concept of tithing to the fore in the last decade, and (4) some of the questions which can be raised concerning tithing.

Tithing may be traced to the very beginnings of history. Egyptians tithed. About 3,000 B.C., Egyptians were giving one-tenth of their spoils of war to their gods. According to Herodotus, Cyrus, king of Persia (538–529 B.C.), on the advice of Croesus, the Lydian king, whom he captured at the battle of Sardis, in Asia Minor, asked his soldiers to devote a tenth of their spoils to Jupiter. Because the gods

WHERE THE CHURCHES STAND ON TITHING

Church body	Organized	Stewardship department organized	Encourages tithing	Officially endorses tithing	When officially endorsed
Adventist					
Seventh-day Adventists	1863	....	Yes	Yes	1863
Assemblies of God	1914	1957	Yes	Yes	1914
Baptist					
American Baptist Convention	1907	c. 1920	Yes	....	....
Free Will Baptists	1727	1948	Yes	Yes	1935
National Baptist Convention of America	1880	None	Yes	Yes	1940
National Baptist Convention, USA, Inc.	....	....	Yes	Yes	....
Southern Baptist Convention	1845	....	Yes	Yes	1894
Brethren					
Church of the Brethren	1719 (US)	1955	Yes	Yes	1944
Christian and Missionary Alliance	1887	None	Yes	Yes	....
Church of Christ	1906	None	No	No	....
Church of God	1880	1938	Yes	Yes	1924
Disciples of Christ	1809	1952	Yes	....	....
Evangelical Mission Covenant	1885	None	Yes	Yes	1942
Friends					
Five Years Meeting of Friends	1902	1955	....	....	....
Religious Society of Friends	1900	None	....	No	....
Jehovah's Witnesses	....	....	No	No	....
Latter-day Saints					
Church of Jesus Christ of Latter-day Saints	....	....	Yes	Yes	1838
Lutheran					
American Lutheran	1930	1934	Yes[1]	No	....
Evangelical Lutheran	1917	....	No	No	....
Lutheran Free Church	1897	1953	Yes	No	....
Lutheran Church—Missouri Synod	1847	....	Yes[1]	No	....
The United Lutheran Church in America	1918	1945	Yes	No	....
Mennonite					
Evangelical Mennonite	1860	None	Yes	Yes	1922
Mennonite Church	1863 (US)	1957	Yes	No	....
Methodist					
Free Methodist Church	1860	1943[2]	Yes	Yes	....
The Methodist Church	1939	....	Yes	Yes	1944[3]
Wesleyan Methodist Church	1843	....	Yes	Yes	1925
Moravian Church in America—Northern Province	1740	....	Yes	Yes	1951

WHERE THE CHURCHES STAND ON TITHING (*Continued*)

Church body	Organized	Stewardship department organized	Encourages tithing	Officially endorses tithing	When officially endorsed
NAZARENE					
Church of the Nazarene	1908	1917	Yes	Yes	1908
ORTHODOX					
Archdiocese of the Greek Orthodox in America	....	....	Yes	Yes	1950[4]
PRESBYTERIAN					
Cumberland Presbyterian Church	1810	1956	Yes	Yes	1957
Presbyterian Church in the U.S.	1861	1910	Yes	Yes	1891
Presbyterian Church in the U.S.A.	1706	1935	Yes	Yes	1951
United Presbyterian Church	1858	1882	Yes	Yes	1865
Protestant Episcopal Church	1789	None	Yes (1957)	Yes	1955
REFORMED					
Reformed Church in America	1628	1952	Yes	Yes	1947
Christian Reformed Church	1857	....	Yes	No	....
Reformed Episcopal Church	1873	....	Yes	No	....
Salvation Army	1865	None	Yes	Yes	1865
United Brethren in Christ	1889	None	Yes	Yes	1889
Unitarian Churches	1825	None	Yes	No	....
Canadian Churches					
Anglican Church of Canada	....	....	Yes	Yes	1952
Maritime United Baptist Convention	....	1955	Yes	....	....[5]
The Presbyterian Church in Canada	....	1947	No	No	....
United Church of Canada	1925	1925	Yes	Yes	1955
Overseas Churches[6]					
ASSAM					
Gossner Evangelical Lutheran	....	....	No	No	....
AUSTRALIA					
Church of England in Australia and Tasmania	....	1957	No	No	....
Congregational Union of Australia	....	....	No	No	....
BELGIUM					
Union of Protestant Evangelical Churches of Belgium	....	None	No	No	....
BRAZIL					
Methodist Church of Brazil	....	....	Yes[7]	Yes	....
BRITISH GUIANA					
Evangelical Lutheran Church	....	....	Yes	Yes	....
CHILE					
German Evangelical Church in Chile	....	....	No	No	....

WHERE THE CHURCHES STAND ON TITHING (*Concluded*)

Church body	Organized	Stewardship department organized	Encourages tithing	Officially endorses tithing	When officially endorsed
Great Britain and Ireland					
Baptist Union of Great Britain and Ireland	....	....	....	No	....
Congregational Union of Scotland	....	....	No	No	....
Scottish Episcopal Church	....	....	Yes	No	....
Holland					
Free Will Baptist Church	....	....	Yes	....	....
India					
Church of South India	....	....	No	No	....
Pentecostal Churches of India	....	....	Yes	....	....
Tamil Evangelical Church of India	....	....	No	No	....
Iran					
Presbyterian Church in Iran	....	....	Yes	....	....
Italy					
Methodist Church of Italy	....	....	No	No	....
Japan					
Evangelical Lutheran Church	....	1956[3]	Yes	No	....
Near East					
Union of the Armenian Evangelical in the Near East	....	....	Yes	No	....
Poland					
Evangelical Church of the Augsburg Confession	....	....	No	No	....
Spain					
Spanish Evangelical Church	....	....	No	No	....
Tanganyika					
Lutheran Church of Northern Tanganyika	....	....	Yes	No	....
Thailand					
Church of Christ in Thailand (Union of Protestant churches)	1934	....	Yes	No	....

[1] Proportionate giving.

[2] "The department of tithing was organized in 1943, and the word 'stewardship' was added in 1951," thus becoming the Department of Stewardship and Tithing.

[3] Note the evolution of tithing: 1939—the Uniting Conference, no mention of tithing in the *Doctrines and Discipline of The Methodist Church;* 1940—"The dedication of the tenth of income offers a basic principle of beneficence supported by centuries of religious custom and joyful experience" (#1249); 1944—"Tithing is commended as a historic and workable method attested by many Christians throughout centuries of religious custom and joyful experience"

were considered partners in battle, it was believed they were entitled to a tithe of the spoil. Cyrus, however, had an ulterior motive—he was afraid that one of his men would gain too many spoils from the city of Sardis and rebel against him. But by claiming all of the tenths in the name of Jupiter, Cyrus knew he would have a total that would exceed the loot claimed by any one man. The custom of giving a tenth to the gods of the ancient world is found also in Babylonia, Arabia, Greece, Rome, and China. Ten, being a basic number, was considered a convenient, if not a mystical, number. Since ten included all the basic digits, it was regarded as standing for totality, and one-tenth for a part of the whole.

Who was the first tither according to the Bible?

Did Cain tithe? Did Abel tithe? Says the writer of Hebrews: "By faith Abel offered unto God a more excellent sacrifice than Cain."[1] John Selden, who opposed the national tithe in seventeenth century England, and who consequently spent many years in the Tower thinking about his position, believed that although the main difference between Cain and Abel's giving was one of quality and attitude, the main difference was in their concept of the tithe. Abel gave a

---

(#223); 1948—no change; 1952—"Stewardship of possessions shall be interpreted to mean that the tithe is the minimum standard of giving for Methodist people, and shall be promoted by the above agencies (Boards of Education and Lay Activities) by providing appropriate literature for the use of churches and pastors in enlisting Methodist people as tithers" (#753); 1956—no change.

[4] At the Greek Orthodox "Laity-Clergymen" convention at St. Louis (Nov. 26–Dec. 1, 1950), the Greek Orthodox Archdiocese established a department of the "Decadollarion" (ten dollars), which handles the dues paid by each member family for the maintenance and work of the Archdiocese.

[5] "Stressed more in the last six years."

[6] Geographical sampling of overseas churches. Excluded are state churches (see page 56), which, primarily because of their share in state taxes, ignore the tithe.

[7] Some churches observe a "tithing" Sunday once a quarter or once a month.

[8] First stewardship conference held.

Sources of information on tithing are from interviews, correspondence with the stewardship or financial officials of the church bodies, consultation with records and published statements of the churches. "Encourages tithing" means encourages tithing in the educational or promotional literature of the church group; "officially endorses tithing" means endorsement by recorded statements or resolutions of the representative body or executive committee of the church.

---

[1] Hebrews 11: 4.

tithe of his best, Cain of his worst. He conjectures that Cain killed Abel because Abel accused him of tithing evil. Such an exegesis is interesting to say the least, but highly dangerous. Purely a fiction, "it is," as another tithing historian, H. W. Clarke, comments on Selden's exegesis, "very wrong that Scriptural passages, such as that given above, should be distorted in order to induce people to pay tithes."[2] A conclusion that Cain and Abel were tithers is purely conjecture. Whether they were or not, of course, cannot be answered categorically, but to state affirmatively that they were tithers, a person has to rely solely on fiction. And, as Clarke also adds, "a good cause needs no fiction to bolster it up."[3]

Abraham is the first person recorded in the Bible as giving tithes. As the king of Elam and his allies were in the process of attacking Sodom and Gomorrah, they raided the camp of Lot, Abraham's brother's son.[4] Lot was taken captive. Hearing this, Abraham recruited his servants and set out angrily to retrieve his relative. Abraham pursues the kings to their death. Returning with Lot, Abraham meets the king of Salem, Melchizedek, whose name has the mysterious meaning of "King of righteousness." Melchizedek blesses him. Then Abraham gives one-tenth "of all" to Melchizedek.

Some critics argue that the incident with Melchizedek is a poetic and symbolic legend; they maintain that the list of the kings in the account conflicts with cuneiform lists and that the route of the king of Elam's army did not allow for the presence of the Dead Sea. But assuming the historical accuracy of the account, we have Abraham giving a tenth of "all." Whether he is giving a tenth of the spoils of war or from all of his possessions we do not know. This is the only mention of his tithing—a tribute in the ancient sense to the successful deity—and no mention of his giving from the regular increase of his herd or crops.

The occasion of Abraham's tithing is mentioned again in the New

[2] Henry Clarke, *A History of Tithes* (New York: Charles Scribner's Sons, 1894), p. 3.
[3] *Ibid.*, p. 9.
[4] Genesis 14.

Testament. Melchizedek is discussed with some detail in the seventh chapter of Hebrews. A list of attributes of Melchizedek is given, and because he possesses a certain reputation Melchizedek becomes an analogy or prototype of Christ. First of all a king of righteousness, he is also called king of Salem, or king of peace.[5] He is such a strange figure, the records point out, that there is no indication of his having a mother or father, nor descendants, nor a beginning of life nor an end.

Since Christ lives forever, is he to receive tithes as the priest Melchizedek did? If Abraham's occasion of tithing is accepted as a standard of practice by the New Testament writer of the Epistle to the Hebrews, then of course tithing could be argued as justifiable for Christians.

But these considerations make it difficult to liken Jesus to Melchizedek at the point of receiving tithes. (1) When Abraham paid tithes he paid them to a visible priest. Jesus did not function as an official priest during his ministry on earth. Not until his atonement did he actually become the mediator. (2) Offerings and gatherings of funds in the New Testament were raised for the glory of God, not dedicated specifically to Jesus. (3) The comparison between Melchizedek and Jesus is not one of ability to collect or expect tithes, but of the fact that both had priestly qualities. Christ was born of a virgin "without priestly descent" also;[6] he is eternal and sits on the right hand of God; he is the high priest, the "king of righteousness" and "king of peace." These are the parallels of the two prototypes.

Tithing for Abraham was a response. It was spontaneous. We have no indication that he ever tithed again or, if he did, that there was any regularity about his procedure. Perhaps his tithing was the result of a custom of his homeland in Ur of the Chaldaeans, or the result of the influence of the Salemite king. All we know is that Abraham returning from war met a priest-like neighboring king and chose on that occasion to give him one-tenth, which the writer of the

[5] Hebrews 7: 2.
[6] Hebrews 7: 13.

Epistle to the Hebrews prefers to define as one tenth of the spoils.[7]

The second tither in the Bible is Jacob who, while fleeing for his life, makes a personal covenant with God. Jacob has just left the sight of his brother Esau and is heading for the land of his mother's father, Laban. Jacob is thoroughly frightened. His fears are aggravated when, as he lies upon the stones to sleep, there come a theophany and the promise, "I am with thee, and will keep thee in all places whither thou goest, and will bring thee again into this land. . . ."[8] Jacob wakes up and exclaims: "How dreadful is this place! this is none other but the house of God."[9] And he proceeds to name the place "house of God," or "Beth-el." Jacob is so pleased with the fact that God is on his side that he immediately strikes a bargain—partly in recognition of God's providential care of him and partly because this shrewd man knows that God is with him and he wants to make the best of the situation. So Jacob says: "Of all that thou shalt give me I will surely give the tenth unto thee."[10] It seems that Jacob had not thought seriously of the idea before, for his promise is incomplete in the sense that it hinges on the future. Nevertheless it seems like a good idea. Whether he originated it himself or got it from his new pagan contacts or from other sources of antiquity, such as his father, Isaac, or his grandfather, Abraham, is not known. At any rate, Jacob became excited about the possibility of such a bargain, and proceeded to make it with God.

Prior to the time of Moses there seems to have been a double tithe in Egypt. Such a tithe was suggested by Joseph to Pharaoh in order to prepare for the famine.[11] Whether the taxation of one-fifth increased or decreased before the birth of Moses cannot be said. As the hardships were multiplied on the Israelites by the Egyptians, perhaps the double-tithe was aggravated to greater proportions.

Later, during the wandering in the wilderness, as the priestly

[7] Hebrews 7: 4.
[8] Genesis 28: 15.
[9] Genesis 28: 17.
[10] Genesis 28: 22.
[11] Genesis 41: 34; 47: 24.

codes (a part of Numbers, Leviticus) and the Mosaic regulations (Deuteronomy) were formulated, the giving of tithes or "tenths" became required of the people.

There were three basic religious tithes:

1. ***For the support of the Levites*** (Numbers 18: 20-32; Leviticus 27: 30-32.). The Levites were not given an inheritance as were the other tribes, for they were to minister to the spiritual needs of the people. A tenth of the agricultural produce[12] and livestock[13] of the other tribes was to go for the support of the Levites. The Levites in turn were to pay a tithe of all they received to support the high priest and his staff.

The Hebrews automatically gave the tenth animal, whether it was good or bad. A test for honesty was included. If a person tried to put a bad one in the place of the good, both animals were to be given.[14]

2. ***For an annual festival*** (Deuteronomy 14: 22-27). Once a year all the people were to give another tithe for the purpose of holding a big festival. The produce or livestock, however, could be converted ahead of time into money which could be used "for whatsoever thy soul lusteth after, for oxen, or for sheep, for wine, or for strong drink, or for whatsoever thy soul desireth. . . ."[15] Thus if a Hebrew lived far away and could not bring the produce because of travel problems or spoilage, he was permitted to sell it and bring the money or other gifts that would contribute to the festival.

3. ***For the care of the poor*** (Deuteronomy 14: 28, 29). Every third year a tithe was gathered for the relief of the poor. The tithes were put together and a feast was held at which the poor, strangers, and the Levites were entertained as guests of honor. This tithe was not designated to go to Jerusalem, but was to be stored in the cities

[12] Numbers 18: 27-30; Leviticus 27: 30.
[13] Leviticus 27: 32.
[14] Leviticus 27: 32-33.
[15] Deuteronomy 14: 26.

where the tribes were to settle. What was left over from the feast was to be used for local charity.

The early Hebrews did not give a tithe. They gave tithes. Every year they were obligated to give two tithes. But on the third year the amount expected was three tithes, or 30 per cent, and yet the tithes were only a part of their giving. Consider the whole gamut of the Hebrew's giving: "And thither ye shall bring your burnt offerings, and your sacrifices, and your tithes, and heave offerings of your hand, and your vows, and your freewill offerings, and the firstlings of your herds and of your flocks."[16] Since the Hebrews did not pay their Levitical tithes on the basis of the firstfruits,[17] the giving of the firstfruits must be separate from the tithes. And "when one tries to comprehend how much of the lamb crop of a given year on our western ranges would be classified according to Old Testament standards as firstlings, the demands upon the Old Testament farmer are staggering."[18]

An attempt has been made by several writers to combine the offering of firstfruits and the three tithes into one. Emil Sehling, professor of ecclesiastical and commercial law at the University of Erlangen, proposed this earlier in the century.[19] But to do so, Sehling had to rely on a manipulation of the documents which make up the Pentateuch. Even if he were to succeed in lumping all of the tithes and offerings and taxes, the value of the Hebrew gift would still exceed 10 per cent when one considers the real value of the firstfruits, the first-born, the first-ripe, or the earliest fruit against the rest of the crop, which normally would diminish in quality and in demand in the Oriental market places. In addition, the practice of the Sabbatical year and the fallowing of the ground caused the legal

[16] Deuteronomy 12: 6.

[17] Leviticus 27: 32.

[18] A. J. Engelbrecht, professor of Old Testament, Wartburg Seminary, Dubuque, Iowa, in a lecture before the annual meeting of the Joint Commission on Stewardship and Benevolence of the National Council of Churches, 1954, in Toronto.

[19] See Emil Sehling's "Tithes," *The New Schaff-Herzog Encyclopedia of Religious Knowledge,* edited by Samuel Macauley Jackson (New York: Funk and Wagnalls Company, 1911), XI, 453.

requirements of Jewish giving to soar above the tithe. However, rather than to manipulate the text and resort to conjecture, most writers on the tithe, from Lansdell to mid-century writers such as Kauffman, Dodd, Thomas, Salstrand, and Moore, concede the multiplicity of tithes and offerings. An exception is Methodist Bishop Costen J. Harrell, who in his stewardship manual *Stewardship and the Tithe*[20] insists that the three tithes represent three stages of development.

There were three other demands for the Hebrews to tithe. In the first place, the tax of the kings was also a tithe. Samuel says, in trying to talk the Hebrews out of asking for a king, "He will take the tenth of your seed, and of your vineyards, and give to his officers, and to his servants."[21] This 10 per cent tax is not the same as the temple, festival, or charity tithes. It is taken for a different purpose, and cannot be identified with the religious tithes. When Hezekiah introduced his reforms,[22] he revived the religious tithes, which were to go to the Levites and not to the palace treasury. If there was to be a royal tax, as Samuel promised, and if Hezekiah was to support his government by taxation, then it was in addition to the religious tithes. This brought the Jews' giving obligations in respect to tithes to 40 per cent. And it did not stop there.

The Jewish Talmud, which is a collection of traditional laws and comments believed to have been spoken to Moses in addition to the written law, recognizes the three basic religious tithes. And it adds another. Within the Talmud are two parts: the Mishna, which is the text, and the Gemara, which comments on the text. Within the Mishna is a book called the "Demai," which discusses the demai or "doubtful" tithe.

Because of the complexities of the details applied to tithing in the Talmud, some of the instructions become cloudy and are in doubt. For example, consider this complicated procedure concerning the purchase of bread: "He who buys bread from a retail bread-seller

[20] New York: Abingdon Press, 1953.
[21] 1 Samuel 8: 15.
[22] 2 Chronicles 31: 4-10.

ought to tithe each loaf. Again, he who buys from a poor man, or even a poor man himself who shall have received pieces of bread or fragments of fig-cake, ought to tithe each piece separately; but in the case of dates or figs the portion due may be taken collectively."[23]

Many Hebrew men, not unlike the typical American male, who has trouble remembering a simple grocery list, had difficulty keeping in mind and applying correctly the minute details of the tithing laws. So in case of doubt, a provision is made for a special tithe, the "demai" tithe. If a man finds food on the road and is not sure whether it has been tithed or not, he should pay a demai tithe; if a person gives food to his mother-in-law to cook and then partakes of it himself, he should pay a demai tithe on it. When in doubt, the answer was the demai tithe. And this fourth religious tithe was not as demanding—it was only 1 per cent, or one-tenth of the one-tenth. The devoted Hebrew's tithing was over the 40 per cent mark.

Americans who say it is difficult to give to the church from what is left of salaries after taxes, or the Englishmen who frown upon the tithe because of the heavy national income tax, ought to consider what the literal-minded Hebrew had left from which to bring a free-will offering to his God after tithing!

Tithing is not mentioned in connection with the great reigns of David and Solomon. But tithing was doubtless in vogue, if not at its peak, as a method of civil taxation and support for the Levites. David's great military campaigns and Solomon's building of the temple, not to mention the many luxuries of the court, were in comparison as staggering as modern budgets dictated largely by the effects of war and inflation. Popularity of religion was at a peak. The number of Levites over thirty years of age alone totaled 38,000; counting them as family units, the figure would reach 200,000 or 300,000.[24] No small amount of taxes and tithes was required to keep such a government and its ecclesiastical organization operating.

[23] Lansdell's explanation of Sections 4, 5, 8, Chapter 5, of the Book of Demai (also called Dammai—pronounced Damay). From Henry Lansdell's *The Sacred Tenth,* I (London: Society for Promoting Christian Knowledge, 1906), 133.

[24] 1 Chronicles 23: 3.

Among the prophets, tithes are mentioned only once, and then in an unpleasant way by the fiery-tongued cattle rancher and orchard owner Amos, who, following a series of tirades against the neighbors of Israel, turns on Israel herself and asks sarcastically that the people continue their punctilious tithing habits and their sinning. He is speaking to a spiritually dead audience. He has just told them that God would take them "away with hooks, and your posterity with fishhooks."[25] With biting irony he adds: "Come to Bethel, and transgress; at Gilgal multiply transgression; and bring your sacrifices every morning, and your tithes after three years; and offer a sacrifice of thanksgiving with leaven, and proclaim and publish the free offerings. . . ."[26]

Tithing is not mentioned again until a number of centuries later when two near contemporaries, one a builder, and the second a prophet, return to the ruins of Jerusalem to begin to restore the city and its holy atmosphere after the captivity. Nehemiah has a charge from the king of Persia to rebuild the Jerusalem walls; Malachi, at the same time or shortly afterward, begins an even greater, if not more hopeless, task, that of rebuilding the faith and morale of a discouraged people. Another prophet, Haggai, encourages the rebuilding of the Temple. Ezekiel, Jeremiah, and the author of the last part of Isaiah do much to keep a spark of hope alive among the people during the transitional period between the exile and the return.

The work of rebuilding the walls has been completed as Nehemiah urges the people to continue following the Levitical codes and in so doing to bring "the tithes of our ground unto the Levites."[27] He points out further that the Levites will continue bringing the tithes, giving them unto "the treasure house" of the Temple. Tithing continues to be basically agricultural, and Nehemiah continues to speak of the tithe in the plural,[28] although he mentions a specific tithe of

[25] Amos 4: 2.
[26] Amos 4: 4, 5.
[27] Nehemiah 10: 37.
[28] Nehemiah 12: 44—"tithes," *ma-'as-roth.*

corn and wine from Judah in his last reference.[29] He also mentions the tithes as separate from the offerings and the firstfruits, as the writer of Deuteronomy did.

The tithing revival seems to have grown cold after the building of the city, its walls and temple, especially if we place Malachi and his remarks on tithing at the time of, or slightly later than, Nehemiah.[30]

The whole nation seems to have shirked its responsibilities. Malachi uses the tithe as a specific talking point. He likens the irresponsibility to robbery. "Will a man rob God? Yet ye have robbed me. But ye say, Wherein have we robbed thee? In tithes and offerings.

"Ye are cursed with a curse: for ye have robbed me, even this whole nation.

"Bring ye all the tithes into the storehouse, that there may be meat in mine house, and prove me now herewith, saith the Lord of hosts, if I will not open you the windows of heaven, and pour you out a blessing, that there shall not be room enough to receive it."[31]

Malachi's comments on tithing are best understood in the context in which he spoke.

Malachi is speaking about a specific point of the church polity of his time. The fact that he mentions tithing does not mean it should be exaggerated above other matters. Malachi is concerned with the whole picture. Other restrictions of the laws, such as keeping the Sabbath, could have been cited. Consider a similar situation today. When a Baptist or Methodist minister rebukes his congregation for not attending Wednesday-night prayer meetings, he is not necessarily holding up prayer meeting as the action par excellence of the week for Christians. He probably means that it is part of a greater picture. The appeal of TV, greater conveniences at home and greater ease and facility in traveling to many and diverse

[29] Nehemiah 13: 12—"tithe," *ma-'asar*.

[30] "The Book of Malachi fits the situation amid which Nehemiah worked as snugly as a bone fits its socket," *International Critical Commentary* (New York: Charles Scribner's Sons, 1912), "Malachi," by John M. P. Smith, page 7.

[31] Malachi 3: 8-10.

places—all of these are changing the spiritual tone of the congregation. The old things of the old-time religion, the prayer meetings, the Amens, the glorious singing, the testimonies are all being neglected—not that they are par excellence in themselves—but that they are a part of an energetic discipline that made spiritual giants out of the earlier pioneers. By singing "Faith of Our Fathers," we earnestly covet the spiritual zeal and disciplines of the past. This was the feeling of Malachi.

Malachi speaks of tithes, recognizing the three basic tithes. He makes this quite clear: "Ye have robbed me . . . in tithes and offerings" (literal Hebrew—"the tithe and the offering"), and more emphatically, "bring the whole tithe into the storehouse."[32]

The plural aspect of giving, according to Malachi, is further heightened by the inclusion of the need for "offerings." The word for "offering" in verse eight is the same one we mentioned in the last chapter in connection with the spontaneous giving of the Hebrews in building the tabernacle.[33] The word *terumah*, meaning "heave offering," applies to the priest's portion of an animal sacrifice with which he went through a rather curious ceremony of lifting it up and down, signifying what is consecrated unto the Lord. The word in verse four is *minchah*, or "meal offering"; a handful of meal was burned upon the altar and the rest consumed by the priest. *Minchah*, used singularly, often is collective, including the whole system of offerings of the Hebrews, which seems to be the context here. Diversity of offerings is emphasized both in the use of *Minchah* and in contrasting it with *terumah*.

The givers of these offerings to the priests were not the Levites, for Malachi is addressing himself to the secular tribe of Judah.[34] These offerings[35] went directly to the priests from people who also paid tithes to the Levites. Perhaps these offerings were the same as the firstfruits offering[36] which went directly to the priests, also apart

[32] Hebrew: *kol-ha-ma-'aser*, "all the tithe." RSV: "the full tithes."
[33] Exodus 35: 5, 21, 24.
[34] Malachi 3: 4.
[35] Deuteronomy 26: 4, 10.
[36] Deuteronomy 12: 6.

from the tithes. God's command through Malachi, then, is for plural giving which includes plural tithes and plural offerings. Malachi was hardly talking about one-tenth.

As in the case of Amos, whose audience was composed of tithers, Malachi's audience may not have been wholly a company of non-tithers. He is not delivering the curse on people who have entirely neglected the precepts of the laws. We do not know the exact make-up of his audience, but his message allows for the fact that each one could have been an arduous tither. "Ye have robbed me" not in failing to tithe but rather "in tithes and offerings." If a Christian takes this verse literally, he can be a tither or even a 30 per cent giver and still be a thorough robber of God.

Why is Malachi so terribly concerned with the payment of tithes? Verse eleven tells us why. God says: "And I will rebuke the devourer for your sakes, and he shall not destroy the fruits of your ground. . . ." Most likely the crops had failed. Whatever the "devourer" is, Malachi interprets it as a curse from God. Remember that the Levites depended on the tithes in order to eat. When the tithes were cut off they were in danger of starvation. There was a moral as well as a religious obligation to support the Levites. This perhaps accounts for the severity of tone in the prophet's book. The reason for the unusual emphasis on tithing (to prevent starvation of a certain class) and source of the tithe (the crops and flocks of nomads) ought to be kept in mind as compared to our mechanized age when concepts of time, money, goals, organization are radically different.

In modern society where concern is felt even for a dog circling the globe in a satellite at a speed of up to twenty thousand miles an hour, the problems of good and evil and of suffering in the world are very acute. God must be fair; he must be ethical. Malachi's estimation of God, however, is not very high. Says Dr. John M. P. Smith in the International Critical Commentary: "The ethical note is wholly lacking."[37] Malachi brings God back down to the tribal level—if they do this for him, then he will do that for them, and

[37] ICC, "Malachi," p. 73.

vice versa. The whole arrangement is on a material plane. The modern man who questions the justice of the tornado, the flood and the hurricane, and the conduct of certain misbehaving Christians, demands more than a God stashed away in an ethereal attic. His God must be just and ethical. God can love and he can suffer, but he must remain just and ethical on all planes.

With Malachi, the Old Testament comes to an end with a curse. And this is natural enough, for man, in all of his weaknesses, can never conform wholly to the laws of God. Through the cycles of a lost desert tribe and its wars, through a period of judges, a monarchy, a divided kingdom and exile and restoration, the children of God kept sinning and returning to their old ways. Truly their righteousness was "as filthy rags."[38] A curse is the natural outcome of the law—not that God erred in sending the law, for it was for the edification of man and the essence of it exists beyond the letter—but man needed more, a savior, an eternal sacrifice, to bring him spotless before God. Thus God meets man in a new covenant of which Malachi (Chapter 4) can give only a hint. Whereas the Old Testament ends with a curse, the New Testament ends with a cross. Malachi speaks of "the great and dreadful day of the Lord"[39] and the warning for the people to be true to their spiritual obligations "lest I come and smite the earth with a curse." [40] The Apostle John in his Apocalypse ends with words of the Savior: "Even so, come, Lord Jesus. The grace of our Lord Jesus Christ be with you all. Amen."[41] Through the law there is a curse, and giving that is shaped by the law cannot escape the pitfalls of the law, but giving under grace escapes the law, becomes new, becomes free. The problem of reconciling the legalism of Malachi with the fact that Jesus has come is not an easy task.

However, the fact that two persons or two ideas are not compatible does not mean that one makes void the other. Jesus was different

[38] Isaiah 64: 6.
[39] Malachi 4: 5.
[40] Malachi 4: 6.
[41] Revelation 22: 20, 21.

from John the Baptist in many respects, but one supplemented the other. One raised a question that prepared the way for the other; one, being the Savior, answered the question which the other raised. Could Jesus, who came not to destroy the law but to fulfill it, also not dispose of the priestly and Mosaic codes, but re-endow them or a part of them, keeping the spirit of the law? Could there be such a thing as Christian tithing?

The whole matter of Christian tithing rises or falls by what Jesus thought or said on the subject. Actually, the matter is not so much concerned with the possibility of a contradiction, for contradiction and paradox are the essence of the spirit and certainly the essence of a creative faith. The point is: How does Jesus meet the matter of a contradiction between a tithe and the gospel? Does tithing become a matter of faith? Does he ignore it? Does he oppose it?

A specific answer is not to be found. Although Jesus, it has been remarked, said more about money than about faith and prayer together, he had nothing to say explicitly about tithing. This silence in regard to defining his position on tithing, however, does not mean that he was a great and careful tither nor does it mean that he did not believe in tithing. Jesus avoided classifications. He came to be the Savior for saints and sinners alike, for tither and non-tither, and since his gospel was timeless, it could not deal specifically with details, including tithing. From the start, then, we cannot hope to find very much to support or condemn tithing or to find an explicit answer in Jesus' teachings. Nevertheless, several questions can be asked to derive a general idea of what Jesus thought of tithing. Did he practice it himself, as a youngster, during the time of his ministry? What was his attitude toward the law of which the tithe is a part? What did Jesus mean when he mentioned the tithe in his rebukes of the Pharisees? Is tithing consistent with Jesus' teachings?

Jesus was brought up in a devout Jewish family; devout Jews gave tithes. Did Jesus therefore tithe? Although the argument is from silence rather than from any known fact, it can be presumed that Jesus tithed as a youngster when he came of age to assume his Jewish responsibilities. He certainly was interested in the holy things of his time—and he showed great respect for the elders and teachers of the temple.[42] Did he continue to give tithes after he was baptized of John the Baptist and as he set forth on his divine ministry? His early vocation changed from carpenter to Messiah and teacher. It is possible that some of his habits and ideas could have changed. So, when asking the question, "Was Jesus a tither?" let us consider the years of his ministry.

However, we must say that even if Jesus had been a rigorous tither during his ministry, it would not have much bearing on Christian procedure, for Christians are neither Jews nor Jesus. What would be true for Jesus as a Jew, as a person out of the past and as the Son of God, does not mean that the same thing would be true for Christians today. For instance, it was Jesus' custom to attend the synagogue on Saturday. Yet we attend church on Sunday. The fact that Jesus attended the synagogue on Saturday does not mean that he recommends that day; it could have been his custom despite the fact that his personal preference might have been Tuesday or Wednesday. What Jesus did according to custom is no yardstick of what he taught.

Nevertheless in Jesus' life, and particularly in his teaching, there is meaning for the Christian, for out of Jesus' living and thinking under the direction of the Father come the disciplines and expectations which he has for his followers. Is there any exemplary action in his life and anything in his teachings that would sanction tithing?

We can look for an answer in the nature of Jesus' vocation, his giving habits, and his attitude toward the law of Israel.

1. As Jesus went about the earth, he had a ministerial or prophetic function. Although he was a religionist, he was not an orthodox one; thus his subsistence came not from tithes. Jesus did not support himself, but depended on the kindness of his friends and the diligence of his apostles. He slept in the open

[42] Luke 2: 46-49.

or in the homes of friends;[43] his food came from the hands of friends and, on occasion, from the use of his miraculous gift. Five loaves and two fishes[44] provided food, after he had blessed them, for a great company, including his own group and presumably himself. And Jesus could not have been a tither—he had no crops, produce, or livestock to market and could not give on the increase of his fields or labors. His relationship to the tithe during his ministry would of necessity be much different from that when he was within the traditional Hebrew philosophy with possibly a regular income of his own in a carpenter shop or some other trade. His idea of money was not bound by natural circumstances.

2. "Take therefore no thought for the morrow" (RSV—"Therefore do not be anxious about tomorrow")[45] was the philosophy by which he taught and lived. When the Romans came inquiring about the tax, Jesus sent Peter to get a coin, not out of a well-planned church or tax budget, but out of the mouth of a fish.[46] Jesus did not think in terms of how much to give, when to give. The reason Jesus did not mention the tithe is not only the fact that he wanted to avoid the details of religious controversy, but also that the proportion and the regularity of his giving were not foremost among his thoughts. Jesus' giving habits were not the most exemplary for the systematic giver. He does not refute systematic nor proportionate giving; but his habits do not give any encouragement to them, if we look to his habits.

3. What about Jesus' concept of the law? If Jesus endorsed any other ideas of proportion in the law, then it would seem tenable that he would endorse the idea of bringing tithes to God, since, as we have seen, the idea could hardly have been foreign to him, a loyal and most energetic Jew in his youth. What about his idea of the Sabbath? If Jesus endorsed proportionate giving of time, then the idea of proportionate giving of money would not be foreign

[43] Matthew 8: 20.
[44] John 6: 5-14.
[45] Matthew 6: 34.
[46] Matthew 17: 27.

to him. What is his attitude toward the Sabbath, or even, for that matter, toward Sunday?

His teaching toward the Sabbath was anything but orthodox. When his disciples proceeded to reap grain in a very limited fashion, but in clear violation of the Sabbath work laws, the Pharisees were startled. But not Jesus. He reminded his critics: "Have ye not read what David did, when he was an hungred . . . how he entered into the house of God, and did eat the shewbread, which was not lawful for him to eat, neither for them which were with him, but only for the priests?"[47] He was like a man coming in off the street on Sunday morning, be it a laborer or the President, and eating the bread off the altar in St. Patrick's in Manhattan and drinking the wine which was only lawful for the priests to drink. Jesus does not hold David up for an example—but exhorts the Pharisees not to worry about it and to mind their chief business of recognizing and exemplifying the mercy and love of God. Jesus permitted his disciples to break the Sabbath laws and he heaped insult upon insult by inferring that there was nothing wrong with eating the elements of the sacrament for breakfast on the Sabbath. Putting tithing in the same category as the Sabbath indeed makes an interesting comparison. In this connection it would be interesting to see what Jesus would say about tithing, if Jesus' interpretation of all matters of the law, including tithing, were to follow his attitude toward the Sabbath.

The logic of the Sabbath is a stumbling block to many stewardship thinkers when they arrive at the brink of deciding for or against tithing. There looms the traditional idea of the Jewish Sabbath. God, it is argued, from the creation of the world ordained that man should rest on the seventh day;[48] the fourth commandment says to remember the Sabbath to keep it holy.[49] Yet Jesus keeps busy with his vocation on the Sabbath, healing and preaching. Says he: "The sabbath was made for man, and not man for the sabbath."[50]

[47] Matthew 12: 3, 4.
[48] Genesis 2: 3.
[49] Exodus 20: 9-10.
[50] Mark 2: 27.

In other words, man is not to be chained down to legalistic observances of the Sabbath. The fact that God rested on the Sabbath does not mean that man has to do so to the point of suspending his normal dedicated activities. Nor do the Ten Commandments bind us to a law of the Sabbath and consequently to other laws of proportionate observances. We do not take any of the Ten Commandments completely literally. We say, "Thou shalt not kill," yet we kill animals and, in war, human beings; we say, "Thou shalt not commit adultery," yet Jesus says that a person who so much as looks on another person lustfully commits adultery;[51] we say, "Thou shalt not steal," yet great church thinkers, such as Aquinas, justified stealing at least in situations of dire emergency and need.[52] With the advent of automation and with new concepts of leisure time arising, it is quite probable that the church's thinking on the practice and observance of one day a week will have to be redefined and worked out on a plane different from that of an early Hebrew tribal agricultural timetable. The Sabbath, as Jesus says, is relevant to man. The same with giving—it is relevant to the man and, in Christianity, to the new man. Resting today is not the same as resting 3,500 years ago—there are psychological rest values in certain types of work, such as cutting the grass, reading, repairing a car, or the pursuit of some other hobby. When compared with the Sabbath, then, even without allowance for the New Covenant, giving would be different today from what it was in early Hebrew history. And if the Sabbath requirement which was among the original commandments received at Sinai is treated independently, if not lightly, by Jesus, what shall we expect of the tithe? If the principal parts of the Covenant code are not binding per se in their literal inception, then how much more binding would be the supplementary laws of ceremonies and practice? Perhaps they too are

[51] Matthew 5: 28.

[52] "If the need be so manifest and urgent . . . then it is lawful for a man to succor his own need by means of another's property, by taking it openly or secretly." From Thomas Aquinas, *Summa Theologica,* Vol. II (Part II, Second Part, Question 66, Seventh Article) (New York: Benziger Brothers, Inc., 1947), p. 1481.

relevant, and subject to reinterpretation and reorientation under grace.

Jesus makes remarks on tithing in two instances—and in both cases in negative exclamations.

Jesus describes one Pharisee as saying, "I fast twice in the week, I give tithes of all that I possess." This man Jesus contrasts to a publican—a sinner—and states that the publican "went down to his house justified rather than the other," the tither.[53]

In Jesus' last public discourse in the Temple court where he gives his blistering denunciation of the habits and attitudes of the Pharisees, he says: "Woe unto you, scribes and Pharisees, hypocrites! for ye pay tithe of mint and anise and cummin, and have omitted the weightier matters of the law, judgment, mercy, and faith: these ought ye to have done, and not to leave the other undone."[54]

Is Jesus then advocating tithing? To the contrary. One Southern Baptist pastor says: "The context requires that we understand the saying as a stricture upon the Pharisees and Scribes and its application is to them, not to Christians, who ought not to be lumped indiscriminately with Pharisees! This is dubious exegesis which violates the context and misses the point of the verse."[55]

Jesus is talking directly to those who are under the law. He is saying that the Pharisees bound by the requirements of the law ought to have observed the tithes in addition to their other legal responsibilities. The Greek in both the Matthew and Luke references is impersonal and in the past, using imperfect and aorist tenses; literally it says, "these things it was necessary to have done," not "these things ought ye to have done." There is no directive from Jesus that Christians under grace ought to give tithes.

There are also some textual difficulties in using this verse as a

[53] Luke 18: 12, 14.

[54] Matthew 23: 23 (see also Luke 11: 42).

[55] Rev. Paul L. Stagg, pastor of the First Baptist Church, Front Royal, Virginia, before a meeting of the Southern Baptist Commission of the Study of the Doctrine of the Church, at Southern Baptist Theological Seminary, Louisville, Kentucky, 1955. The same statement appears, in essence, in *What Is the Church?*, edited by Duke K. McCall (Nashville: Broadman Press, 1958), Chap. 9, "An Interpretation of Christian Stewardship," by Paul L. Stagg, p. 152.

prooftext. Codex Bezae (D), one of the more important of the early manuscripts of the New Testament, in addition to the inconclusive redaction of Marcion, deletes the remark about "these things ought ye to have done" in the Luke version. Curiously, these two sources transpose it to the end of verse 41. It thus reads, "But rather give alms of such things as ye have; and behold, all things are clean unto you. These things ought ye [it was necessary] to have done, and not to leave the other undone. But woe unto you, Pharisees! for ye tithe mint and rue and all manner of herbs, and pass over judgment and the love of God. Woe unto you Pharisees. . . ."

Textual criticism opens the matter more widely. But it is not necessary. The context of the verse eliminates it as a single prooftext for tithing.

What did the early Christians and Paul say about tithing? The matter is categorically simple. They said nothing, absolutely nothing. Peter, Paul, John, James, and all the rest of the leaders of the early church probably tithed in their earlier days to whatever extent practices of the Mosaic law were observed in the days of foreign suppression and heavy taxation. Paul, it probably would be safe to say, was a tither at least prior to his conversion. He was a "Hebrew of the Hebrews,"[56] who as a Jewish official had an interest in the strict observances of the law. Even after his conversion he had a hard time getting rid of the influence of the law. For although he would not circumcise Titus,[57] he preferred to circumcise Timothy, his son in the spirit.[58] He went to Jerusalem because he was under a vow[59] and was determined to be there at Pentecost.[60] Nevertheless, in spite of certain affections for the old law, Paul became its most bitter critic. It was Paul who stood up against the first of the apostles, Peter, when Peter began to side with messengers sent by James and to lapse into the old habits.[61] So forcible were the Judaizers that they seem to have reconverted or reori-

[56] Philippians 3: 5.
[57] Galatians 2: 3.
[58] Acts 16: 3.
[59] Acts 18: 18.
[60] Acts 20: 16.
[61] Galatians 2:4ff.

entated all of the brethren to the old ways except Paul, who said: "When I saw that they walked not uprightly according to the truth of the gospel, I said unto Peter before them all, If thou, being a Jew, livest after the manner of Gentiles, and not as do the Jews, why compellest thou the Gentiles to live as do the Jews?"[62]

For Paul the division between law and grace is acute. "For Christ is the end of the law for righteousness to every one that believeth," said Paul. It is that severe with Paul. It was not Paul who said, "Faith, if it hath not works, is dead."[63] But rather he said: "For by grace are ye saved through faith; and that not of yourselves: it is the gift of God: not of works, lest any man should boast."[64] Paul is an extremist when it comes to Christian faith, although he regards the law as a "schoolmaster" (King James) or "custodian" (RSV) until Christ came. "We are no longer under a schoolmaster,"[65] he says. He was so steeped in the law that he was spiritually blind to Christ until Christ revealed himself to him. Paul was so relieved with his new faith that he wanted to put the "old man"[66] as far away from him as he could. He knew what Jesus meant when he said: "Her sins, which are many, are forgiven; for she loved much: but to whom little is forgiven, the same loveth little."[67] A terrible weight was taken from Paul in his new birth, and this weight was the law. We of course cannot argue from silence and say that Paul was diametrically opposed to tithing. Since he does not mention it even by inference, we cannot speak for him. But we do know what he thought of the old life and the old law of which tithing was a part. "But that no man is justified by the law in the sight of God, it is evident: for, The just shall live by faith. And the law is not of faith: but, The man that doeth them shall live in them. Christ hath redeemed us from the curse of the law, being made a curse for us. . . ."[68]

[62] Galatians 2: 14.
[63] James 2: 17.
[64] Ephesians 2: 8, 9.
[65] Galatians 3: 24, 25.
[66] Romans 6: 6.
[67] Luke 7: 47.
[68] Galatians 3: 11-13.

Concerning the new life and the new covenant, Paul had said earlier, in Galatians: "I am crucified with Christ: nevertheless I live; yet not I, but Christ liveth in me: and the life which I now live in the flesh I live by the faith of the Son of God, who loved me, and gave himself for me.

"I do not frustrate the grace of God: for if righteousness come by the law, then Christ is dead in vain."[69] Whether Paul was for tithing, against it, or indifferent to it, his contribution to the subject must be considered in the light of his intense feeling of the differences between law and grace. His premise concerning giving and his measurement of giving would have to be in the light of grace.

Christians of the first two centuries of the Christian era were certainly conscious of the Old Testament customs of tithing, but they did not heed them. "In the intensity of their faith, they did not limit themselves to the fraction of a tenth but gave more generously of their possessions to the clergy and their poorer fellows."[70] "It is admitted universally that the payment of tithes, or the tenths of possessions, for sacred purposes did not find a place within the Christian church during the age covered by the apostles and their immediate successors."[71] Giving, according to Irenaeus (A.D. 120–202), was not determined by proportionate measurement, such as the tithe. It was measured by the cross. "They [the Jews] had indeed the tithes of their goods consecrated to Him, but those who have received liberty set aside all their possessions for the Lord's purposes bestowing joyfully and freely . . . since they have the hope of better things."[72] The early Christian's giving resembled more the communal and the enthusiastic sharing of the Essenes who had their headquarters, it seems, very close to the nerve center

[69] Galatians 2: 20-21.

[70] Catherine Boyd, *Tithes and Parishes in Medieval Italy* (Ithaca, New York: Cornell University Press, 1952), p. 26.

[71] J. R. Willis, "Tithes," in *Dictionary of the Apostolic Church*, I, edited by James Hastings (New York: Charles Scribner's Sons, 1922), 594.

[72] Alexander Roberts and W. H. Rambaut, translators, *The Writings of Irenaeus*, "Against Heresies," Book IV, Chap. XVIII (Edinburgh: T. and T. Clark, 1868), I, 432.

of Palestine in the rugged countryside less than twenty miles southeast of Jerusalem.

But suddenly in the last part of the third century, and in the first part of the fourth century, the idea of tithing burst forth. The support was at first more academic than official. Although the first Christian emperor, Constantine, continued various forms of Roman land tithes and taxes, he issued an edict in 322 which gave full liberty to his subjects to determine the size of the portion that they should give to the clergy.[73] The church fathers now, however, began to back tithing. Cyprian, Ambrose, Augustine, Jerome, and Chrysostom all spoke out for tithing. The reason for this change of attitude, Boyd believes, was a growth in the number of clergy and the conversion of large groups of the poor in the cities. Since the Old Testament ecclesiastical tithes existed primarily for two purposes, the support of the clergy and the care of the poor, tithing was a natural plan. It caught on like fire. A debate began to rage as to which was the more important in the distribution of the tithes—the support of the clergy or the care of the poor. It seems that the second interpretation won out. "Caesarius of Arles went so far as to affirm that the Christian who failed to pay tithe was guilty of the death of the poor."[74]

Four developments brought tithing from obscurity in the early history of the church into full blossom in the pre-medieval period.

In 567 the Synod of Tours met in Gaul and recommended that the Christians in the province should donate to the church one-tenth of their property, which included their slaves. The money from the tithes was to go to the benefit of the poor and as ransom money for captives.

Eighteen years later, in 585, the second council of Macon changed the tithe into a church tax, making non-payment of the tithe punishable by excommunication. These councils were merely local meetings, but they pointed to the direction in which the church was heading in regard to the tithe.

[73] Clarke, *A History of Tithes,* p. 7.
[74] Boyd, *op. cit.,* p. 28.

Two popes did much to pave the way of the tithe. The first is Pope Leo the Great (440–461), the second is Gregory the Great (540–604). Leo appointed certain days on which the faithful brought offerings to be used for the benefit of the poor. The offering, in which the entire locale shared, was called a *collectio,* or collection, and was voluntary. However, during the pontificate of Gregory the Great, the *collectio* gave way in certain areas, such as Rome and Genoa, to a compulsory tax. Old church papers, Boyd points out, show that a blind man in 599 appealed for clemency from Gregory the Great in paying the compulsory church tax.[75] Gregory began to use interchangeably the word *decima,* a tenth, with the word *collectio* (also *collatio*). The use of *decima,* however, was more allegorical than literal, Boyd explains. Gregory used it to mean an offering in general.[76] Nevertheless, regardless of what Gregory meant by the use of *decima,* he showed an acquaintance with the tithing law of the Levites. Leo and Gregory introduced both the mentality and the terminology for a revival of tithing in the established church.

Finally, pressure for tithing came from the outposts of Europe. If one may assume the authenticity of a book, *Penitential,* in part ascribed to Archbishop Theodore of Canterbury, tithing was a habit among the English people at the end of the seventh century. Theodore's regulations on tithing eventually influenced the Irish, and in the eighth century the Irish church canons reflected various instructions on paying the tithe and were circulated widely on the Continent.

When the practice of the tithe began to sweep back into Italy with the conversion of the Lombards, who seem to have acquired the idea from their neighbors to the north—Britain, Gaul, Germany—it differed from Gregory's compulsory *collectio* or *decima.* The concept of the *decima* from the north remained voluntary. Those who gave a tenth received special merit, but there was no compulsion to pay a tenth.

[75] *Ibid.,* p. 31.
[76] *Ibid.,* p. 32.

All Europe was now on the threshold of the tithe. The practice of the tithe became compulsory with the conquest of Italy by the Frankish king Charlemagne. His father, Pippin, had made an ecclesiastical tithe mandatory in all of the Frankish territory. Charlemagne continued the policy over his vast domains, which included France, Belgium, Holland, half of modern Germany, Austria, Hungary, more than half of Italy, and part of northeastern Spain. With Charlemagne in the ninth century the tithe became civil law in the West.

Three developments during the reign of the Carolingian kings won a larger place for the tithe in the thinking and canons of the church and also shaped the character of the tithe in the Middle Ages.

1. ***The secularization of the tithe.*** Charles Martel and his successors, Pippin and Charlemagne, began giving kickbacks from church property to the laymen who provided troops for the royal campaigns. Charles Martel had hoped to make restitution later to the churches. But the continued campaigns of his successors made this impossible. In order to pay back the church centers (abbeys, and so on), he taxed the lay holders of church property a double tithe—a *decima* and a *nona,* a tenth and a ninth. This arrangement put the collection of the tithe into the hands of laymen. When the laymen began to erect their own churches on their own estates, contention arose as to whom the people should pay the tithes—the bishoprics or local chapels—and who should administer the tithes, the church or the laymen.

It was not until 1078 that the question concerning the powers of the laymen over the tithe was settled. Hildebrand, who became Pope Gregory VII, had fanatical designs for the power of the papacy, as did the German king Henry IV. When Henry, without the Pope's permission, appointed an archbishop of Milan, the action infuriated Hildebrand. Henry was speedily cited to Rome by the Holy See to answer for his conduct, to which request Henry retorted that Hildebrand was "not pope but a false monk," and told him to "descend, descend, to be damned throughout the ages."[77] Henry discovered that the empire was not united behind him, and decided that he would have to have the absolution of the church, which would give him the necessary political support. Therefore he went to the castle at Canossa where the pope was staying, and appeared on three successive days barefooted in the snow. After Henry received forgiveness, he pursued his military career with great zest, but not without paying a great price. After the humiliation of Henry, the Concordat of Worms in 1122 ended the struggle between the papacy and the empire in favor of the papacy. The spiritual responsibilities of the church, as well as the collection of the revenues, were now in the hands of the church. This did not, however, change the methods of collection or kickbacks, as indicated by the double tithe and other divisions of the revenues which developed, but simply transferred the responsibility of collecting and designating the tithes to the church. The abuses which adhere to a compulsory system of taxation, with divided responsibility of collection and the split designation, now passed over to the church.

2. ***Feudalization of the tithe.*** Tithes were a part of the feudalistic system which Charlemagne incorporated into his government and which by his union of church and state he delivered in essence to the church.

The philosophy of feudalism stemmed basically from the old Roman Empire where the common people had patrons among the politically elite and where there was a mutual exchange of favors —one granting protection and certain reforms, the other granting political support or patronage. Also under the old Roman system a person could lease a piece of land to another party as a token of friendship or as a reward, with no intention of receiving income on it. In such an arrangement, the lessee had no rights against the owner. These two ideas—patronage and granting a lease—were to

[77] Ernest F. Henderson, *Select Historical Documents of the Middle Ages* (London: G. Bell and Sons, Ltd., 1925), p. 373.

have a bearing on the formation of feudalism. Added to these two Roman ideas were the Frankish feeling of a strong tie of loyalty between the vassal and the lord and the ceremonies of feudal homage or oath taking. But the most important factor in the growth of the feudal system was the individual's need for protection.

As late as 846, St. Peter's in Rome was sacked by the raiding Saracens. The need for protection was to continue beyond the Carolingian kings. There developed the need for protection from the empire itself and later from the church. But the Carolingian kings emphasized the need for protection against the barbarians, and brought recognition of feudalism from the state as the accepted social and economic relationship among the people of the domain. Tithes, being an integral part of the feudal system, therefore came into the church by way of the political feudal system which was wed, at least in principle, with the church on Christmas day, 800, when the Frankish king Charlemagne was crowned by the hand of Pope Leo III.

3. ***The papal forgeries and the tithe.*** During the reign of Charlemagne, the church began to react against the power invested in the state, and immediately after Charlemagne's death a movement arose to concentrate greater authority in the church, namely, in the hands of the pope. Thus the Carolingian period set the scene for several phenomenal forgeries that were to be used to give credence to the preeminence and the power of the pope and, by bolstering the morale of the papacy, to pave the way for a strong ecclesiastical administration of the tithe. The *Pseudo-Isidorian decretals,* supposed to have been collected primarily by the seventh century Spanish bishop Isidore of Seville, recorded decisions of popes and councils from Clement of Rome in the first century to Gregory II in the eighth century. They were partly genuine and partly forged. The *Donation of Constantine* also traced the continuity of the Western church to the first "pope," Peter. These forgeries passed as genuine until the fifteenth century when Lorenzo Valla in 1440 finally demonstrated them to be false. Nevertheless the

forgeries armed the pope with sufficient "evidence" to ensure the eventual investiture of power of the empire in the church and primarily in the Holy See at Rome.

Another forgery, *The Constitutions of the Apostles,* believed to have been concocted about A.D. 1000, not only bolstered the claims of the papacy but also directly bolstered the collection of tithes. It was accepted as genuine, even by the canonists of the church, until the late tenth and eleventh centuries. *The Constitutions* stated that the early Christians paid tithes to the apostles. "The fifth canon ordained that first fruits and tithes should be sent to the house of the bishops and priests, and [were] not to be offered upon the altar."[78] The forgeries arising out of the Carolingian period boosted both the authority of the papacy and the right of the church to collect the tithes.

From the firm establishment of the authority of the papacy in the twelfth century, the history of the tithe is unfortunate. Both in Roman Catholic and non-Roman Catholic—Reformation and post-Reformation—instances, where the tithe was carried over from a church to a secular tax, the tithe in the hands of a feudalistic authority became synonymous with abuse.

As the clergy became fabulously rich, the collection of ecclesiastical tithes lost its purpose. Both in the Old Testament and in the pre-medieval church, tithes were received for the purpose of supporting the clergy and helping the poor. Martin Luther's famous ninety-five theses cited the extent to which the original idea of the tithes had been perverted: "The Pope's riches at this day far exceed the wealth of the richest millionaires . . . cannot he therefore build one single basilica of St. Peter out of his own money rather than out of the money of the faithful poor?"[79]

The abusive use of the tithe accounts for the eclipse of the tithe in all three main aspects of Western religion—Judaism, Protestant-

[78] Clarke, *A History of Tithes,* p. 5.

[79] *The Ninety-Five Theses* (Number 86) as quoted in Henry Bettenson's *Documents of the Christian Church* (New York: Oxford University Press, 1943), p. 267.

ism and, strangely enough, Roman Catholicism itself, the area of the original abuse of the tithe in the Christian era.

1. ***The Hebrews reject tithing.*** When the Temple was destroyed in A.D. 70, with it went the whole priestly arrangement which demanded the tithes for the support of the Levites and priests. But a second reason why the Jews have not renewed the tithing plan can be found in the long history of their persecution. Even in Jesus' day it was hard for the Jew to be faithful in all of his tithes and offering obligations. He had taxes to pay to the oppressor, too. The fact that Zacchaeus and Matthew were unpopular as tax collectors can be seen not only in their unholy dealings with the gentiles, but in the fact that they were emissaries of a double taxation. In the Middle Ages the place of the tithe in the persecuting church no doubt helped to sour the Jew further on any renewal of the tithe. Pope Innocent III chided the king of France for giving too much liberty to the Jews. At the council of Oxford which the newly appointed archbishop of Canterbury, Stephen Langton, summoned in 1223, several decrees were passed forbidding the Jews to keep any Christian servants and prohibiting their building any new synagogues. At the Fourth Lateran council eight years earlier in Rome, it was agreed that the Jews were to be held to the payment of the tithe of their produce and the church taxes. "Above all things, they were to be compelled to wear on the breast the disgraceful badge, a woolen stripe four fingers long and two broad, of a color different from the dress."[80] Punishment for a certain deacon of the church who became a Jew was death at the stake. What Jew in the thirteenth century could have a favorable disposition to tithing? Such abuses added their imprint to the heritage of Jews. Rabbi Wolfe Kelman, executive secretary of the Rabbinical Assembly of America, tells me that today he is not "aware of any Jewish congregations which use the tithing method of fund raising" in the sense that every member of the congregation is asked to

[80] H. Graetz, *History of the Jews* (Philadelphia: Jewish Publication Society of America, 1894), III, 516.

give 10 per cent of his income for the synagogue. An examination of records at the Jewish Theological Seminary, New York City, indicates that most Jewish activities are financed by tuition fees, philanthropic gifts, membership dues, central fund-raising campaigns, with no mention of tithing.

2. *The reformers reject tithing.* Adding to the economic and religious turmoil in Europe at the dawn of the sixteenth century was the abusive and exacting collection of the tithes. "The peasantry in general were in a state of economic unrest, not the least of their grievances being the tithes and fees collected by the local clergy."[81] The attitude of the reformers toward tithing was a natural one at the time. Generally the abuses of the Catholic church had been so great that, as Merrill Moore of the Southern Baptists says, the reformers "leaned over backward to avoid the appearance of Catholic greed and money-grabbing. They opposed the tithe because the tithe they knew was a caricature of biblical stewardship."[82] "Luther generally approved the payment of tithes and, in view of their practical convenience, regarded them as the most expedient form of taxing. In Luther's opinion, tithes were to be paid to the temporal sovereignty; but in this he was not seconded."[83] While the rebellious German peasants did not deny the obligation of tithing in their twelve articles of 1525, the Anabaptists spoke out that Christians owed "neither interest nor tithes."[84] Tithing was not rediscovered by the reformers or reaffirmed explicitly as an ecclesiastical institution, but rather was put aside along with the financial philosophy of the Roman church or, in the cases of the state churches, retained as a state or secular tax. Later church leaders, such as John Wesley, opposed the tithe on Biblical and spiritual, as well as ecclesiastical, grounds. "I do not say, Be a good

[81] Williston Walker, *A History of the Christian Church* (New York: Charles Scribner's Sons, 1918), p. 335.

[82] Merrill Moore, *Found Faithful* (Nashville, Tennessee: Broadman Press, 1953), p. 52.

[83] Emil Sehling, "Tithes," *The New Schaff-Herzog Encyclopedia of Religious Knowledge*, XI, 455.

[84] *Ibid.*

Jew; giving a tenth of all you possess," said Wesley. "I do not say, Be a good Pharisee; giving a fifth of all your substance. I dare not advise you, to give half of what you have; no, nor three quarters; but all! Lift up your hearts, and you will see clearly, in what sense this is to be done. . . ."[85]

3. ***The Roman Catholic Church rejects tithing.*** Although canon law (canons 1496, 1502) of the Roman Catholic Church endorses tithing as an obligation for its people, the requirement remains "very much a hypothetical law." The renewal of tithing by ecclesiastical law makes it binding on Catholics, even though Catholics maintain that "the judicial determination of the method and amount, while retaining a figurative value, ceased to have legal force for Christians."[86] A Catholic editor in Chicago says that as far as he knows, in English-speaking countries the Catholic clergy receives no tithes. What is the reason for this reversal in Catholic history and canon law?

The influence of intellectualism (namely, the schoolmen, such as Thomas Aquinas, in the thirteenth century) and the enlightenment of the eighteenth century worked against the tithe.

Although Aquinas discusses to a great extent the obligation to pay tithes,[87] he approaches the subject with considerable openmindedness for his time. He leaves it to the legislation of the Church to say whether it is binding or not. As long as tithing can serve a legitimate purpose, without abuse, Aquinas is for its continued practice. Aquinas takes tithing out of its original legalism and makes it relevant to the discretion of the church. Thus when the two following developments occurred, the Roman Catholic Church, which was not bound theologically to Old Testament and Jewish legalism, faced other alternatives to giving.

Anti-clerical revolutions, such as the Reformation and the French

[85] From "The Danger of Riches," *Arminian Magazine,* 1781.

[86] "Obligation of Contributing to Support of Church," *Clergy Review,* Vol. 40, 1955, pp. 540, 541.

[87] *Summa,* Part II, Second part, Question 87, "Of Tithes," in four articles, pp. 1561-66.

Revolution, gave church tithing severe blows. When the remnants of feudalism in the French church and outside were swept away by the legislation of the French National Assembly on the night of August 4, 1789, the tithe was automatically abolished in France. When the Kingdom of United Italy was launched in 1861, the church tithe had already been abolished over most of the provinces of Italy. A law of 1887 put an end generally to ecclesiastical tithes in Italy, keeping such taxation or rent fees as necessary to avoid total confiscation of church property. Intellectual and political circumstances forced tithing out of the practical arena of the church.

The church found it could get along without tithes. The loss of tithes in Catholic nations forced the Church to find other sources of income. "In most Catholic countries the loss of tithes was compensated by funded endowments, or state pensions and subsidies, so adequately indeed that in France, for example, when the tithe law was dropped from the catechism list of chief commandments for the Church, no other positive injunction was formulated to replace it."[88] In the United States the Catholic Church raises funds primarily from collections during mass, pew rent, stipends for masses, spontaneous offerings, contributions for special services of the church such as baptisms, marriages, funerals.

The abuses which became attached to tithing in a feudal society returned to haunt the Roman Catholics as the old feudal mentality manifested itself in part in the new churches. With the dissolution of the Holy Roman Empire, new state churches were established. In England, Henry VIII both confiscated church property and took over the receipt of the tithes previously controlled by the pope. Today there are sixteen[89] countries in which the church is still linked constitutionally with the civil government. A Lutheran stewardship leader, recently returned from directing pilot stewardship

[88] "Obligation of Contributing to Support of Church," *Clergy Review,* Vol. 40, 1955, p. 540.

[89] Bolivia, Colombia, Costa Rica, Denmark, Dominican Republic, England and Wales, Finland, Greece, Iceland, Italy, Norway, Paraguay, Peru, Scotland, Spain, Sweden (from "State Churches Pay Price for Prestige," by the author in the *Christian Advocate,* Feb. 11, 1954).

projects in Europe, estimates that 30 per cent of the giving is from free-will offerings in Lutheran state-church countries, with most of the rest coming from state taxes.

State churches of Europe think in terms of a tax. Even when tithing is mentioned to their leaders, it is regarded merely as a part of their tax history.

"We had earlier tithing in the Middle Ages, but now we have a church-rate, which is obligatory for all members in our church," says Miss Eira Paunu, Chairman of the Women's Council of the National (Lutheran) Church of Finland. In the National (Lutheran) Church of Iceland, "tithing was practiced in various forms by our church from about 1100 to 1907," says Bishop Asmundur Gudmundsson. "Since then the ministers are paid by the government."

In Norway, "some special form of tithing was given (or taken!) by the state as late as 1848," says Bishop Eivind Berggrav, former president of the World Council of Churches. "The main reason why tithing was discontinued after the Reformation was that tithing had become a sort of *state taxation*."

The abuses which helped to cause the Reformation were to continue in state churches. The Roman Church, which had initiated the ecclesiastical tithing abuses to begin with, was to find itself in turn abused. This was certainly not to be without its psychological effect on the Roman Church even to the present century. The Reverend E. J. Quigley, writing in *The Irish Ecclesiastical Record* earlier in this century, said: "Arthur Young wrote in his Travels that tithes were never extracted anywhere with such 'horrid greediness' as in England. At the time he had not seen Irish tithe gathering. It appalled him. Cobbett, a Protestant, tells how the English parsons tithed and themselves administered corruptly the law to those who refused to pay." One non-conformist, Jeremiah Dodsworth, refused to pay the thirteen pounds ascribed to him in Lockington, Yorks, in 1833. He was without goods or funds. "They sentenced him to three months in gaol! Things were not better in Ireland; small tithes were sued for everywhere." They argued over the digging and tithing of potatoes. Says Mr. Quigley: "Critics of Medieval inquisitor methods seem never to have heard of the tithe courts in Ireland. Into those courts the reverend tithe—the turf shepherds—drove their unwilling Papist victims."[90]

The history of the tithe in the Christian church in the last fifteen hundred years had degenerated from Leo the Great's collection for the poor to a state income tax, with fractions going to the church. Tithing had all but faded out when suddenly it began to bud in the last century on a voluntary and experimental basis and then in this century blossomed as the standard for giving among the majority of United States Protestants.

The modern emphasis on tithing originating spontaneously in the United States has no direct connection with the legal tithes of the Levites or the feudalistic tithes of the Middle Ages. The Jewish tithe was a multiple tithe and was compelled under law. The historical tithe was an unholy blend of ecclesiastical compulsion and secularism. Today's tithe is none of these, but a singular, voluntary church tithe. Rather than to look for links with the Bible and with the history of tithing, links which are more semantical than historical, we shall look for the undercurrents, the elements of modern faith and society, that bring tithing to the forefront today. Tithing has been a growing thing, not stemming directly from history or from revelation.[91]

In the nineteenth century a more secure basis was needed for the financing of the church in order to keep pace with the new mission work and with the growing economy which from 1848 to 1858 received a 400-million-dollar shot in the arm from the California gold rush. Methods were needed both to tap fully the new money for the church and to meet the new obligations of the mission-minded church. While tithing did not become dominant in the nineteenth century, patterns of giving did become more systematic. Societies were organized to encourage systematic giving.

[90] Edward Quigley, "The Sacred Tenth," in *The Irish Ecclesiastical Record* (Browne and Nolan, Limited, Dublin, 1932), p. 612.

[91] Mormons take exception to this. According to the *Doctrine and Covenants of the Church of Jesus Christ of Latter-day Saints* (Section 119), a law of tithing was given by revelation to Joseph Smith at Far West, Missouri, July 8, 1838.

Among these were the Systematic Benevolence Committee of the Old School Presbyterians, organized in 1858. When the Northern (American) Baptists held their first conference on Systematic Beneficence nearly a half century later in the fall of 1896, tithing was a new and exciting subject for them. One of the older pastors, the Reverend M. H. Bixby, of the Cranston Street Church, Providence, challenged the young men to try the idea which he said he had been using personally for twenty-five years. The official program, however, dealt with general subjects such as "A woman's responsibility in the Christian distribution and use of the household income," "Spiritual returns from missionary investments," "Perils of unconsecrated wealth." However, several denominations and religious groups in addition to the Mormons were practicing tithing as early as 1865.[92]

The idea of setting a minimum amount of giving at 10 per cent did not really catch fire until the laymen got hold of the idea. Shortly after the Civil War a Chicago businessman, Thomas Kane, began tithing his personal income. Around 1880 he began to talk with others who had been practicing this method. They shared his enthusiasm and convictions. Mr. Kane began printing pamphlets on tithing, bombarding primarily evangelical ministers in the United States. Later he discovered the existence of a tithing organization, "The Tenth Legion," named after Caesar's most loyal legion, organized by the New York City Union in 1896. Thomas Kane lent his endeavors to the group, which was taken over and revitalized by the United Society of Christian Endeavor in 1897, and in four years (1898–1902) the "legion" grew from 5,000 to 18,500 members. In 1904, with Kane as chairman, another tithing group was organized called "The Twentieth Century Tithers' Association of America." Before his death, Kane organized a non-profit corporation in Chicago, The Layman Company, to carry on his program of tithing. Today, in a little cubbyhole of an office on the sixth floor of 8 South Dearborn, Chicago, the work of Thomas Kane is being continued by a distinguished Presbyterian minister, J. W. McClenahan.

[92] United Presbyterians, Seventh-day Adventists, Salvation Army.

Retired from the active ministry for twelve years, Mr. McClenahan works a regular forty-hour shift for the Layman Tithing Foundation, as the company is now known, and sends out personally 2,000,000 different items on tithing a year. But this was nothing like the volume that the organization used to send, Mr. McClenahan explains. The reason is quite clear. Mr. McClenahan says that the "denominations who used not to say anything about it" have taken tithing over and now make it a part of their own programs and publish highly attractive literature. Mr. McClenahan personally recalls that as a minister fifty years ago he did not say much about tithing. "But it was different after the laymen got hold of it," he says. Tithing, properly considered in United States history, must be dated to a large extent in terms of B.K., and A.K., "before Kane" and "after Kane."

The influence of the philosophy of the pragmatists ("If it works, it's true") on the American mind created a climate for the nourishment of tithing. The most famous of the American pragmatists was William James, whose great interest in religion, as well as in philosophy and medicine, influenced the Protestant church directly through such books as *The Will to Believe* (1897) and *The Varieties of Religious Experience* (1902). Two other pragmatists, F. C. S. Schiller, and particularly John Dewey, were to carry on the torch of pragmatism with a scientific interest that was to influence education. Thus when it was discovered by individuals that tithing brought certain satisfactions, and by churches that it brought great success to the financial program of the church, the Protestant mind, greatly influenced by the scientific, practical philosophy of William James, was fertile for Kane's bombardment of the churches with tithing literature.

Theology also was providing ready ground for tithing. At the turn of the century a young concert organist, who had turned to medicine and to theology, published his *The Quest of the Historical Jesus*, a study of nineteenth century continental thinkers and their views of Jesus and his consciousness of his mission. With Albert Schweitzer's monumental book, which introduced the term *Interim-*

ethik, or "interim ethics," to the West, an influence was introduced into theology which was to help condition it for tithing. In presenting the views of men who suggested that Jesus was laboring under a delusion before he finally faced the cross—the delusion that the Kingdom of God was at hand and the reign of earthly powers was about over—Schweitzer paved the way for the view that Jesus' ethical theology as found in the Sermon on the Mount, for instance, did not necessarily apply to present-day Christians. This, however, was not Schweitzer's own view, but rather the misunderstanding which influenced the theology of certain denominational writers and popular theologians. Jesus, since he was expecting the end, gave the Sermon which was all idealistic, characterized by nonviolence and perfection. When Jesus changed his mind and faced the cross following the Confession of Peter at Caesarea Philippi, all the preceding ethical material was void. Jesus had new things to say—there was to be no short interim, but a long period before the realization of the Kingdom. Schweitzer believes that the interim is still here. Those who refer to Schweitzer, misunderstanding him, say the interim came to an end and so did the harsh ethic Jesus proposed in that period. Christian giving, then, is not seen in a perspective of totality or destiny. A tithe becomes an adequate gift when viewed apart from the interim or eschatological ethics of Jesus.

Following Schweitzer came the defenders of the social gospel such as Walter Rauschenbusch, Shailer Mathews, J. B. Bury, and others who generally bypassed the details of textual criticism and dealt primarily with interpreting the gospel in relationship to current political and economic philosophies, such as Marxism, socialism, capitalism. Critical Biblical exegesis and theology began to wane. The volumes of exegetical, textual studies accessible to the general student were published forty or fifty years or more ago with the new *Interpreter's Bible* the only major exception in about fifty years, and it is more homiletical than critical. This lack of emphasis on Biblical exegesis has carried over into the schools today. In many seminaries Biblical exegetical studies are being crowded out. Especially is this true of the Biblical languages in American Baptist and Methodist schools. The result of the swing to more practical courses has its advantages in adapting the minister to the tremendous tasks and problems of the ministry. But the practical emphasis prepares the minister to accept at face value the various translations of the Scriptures which he has, and leads him to accept a current fad such as tithing without a critical or careful examination of the Scriptures on his own part. With a more vigorous Biblical scholarship on the part of the individual there would be less conformity on Biblical subjects.

The postwar return to security and stability both in the twenties[93] and in the late forties invited tithing. The postwar slogans of the nation's two largest church groups—for example, the slogan of the Joint Centenary Stewardship Department for United States Methodism's (Methodist Episcopal Church and Methodist Episcopal Church, South) centennial celebration, 1919–1923—"A Million Tithers in Methodism," and the Southern Baptist's slogan in 1948, "Every Baptist a Tither"—indicate "postwar" thinking in regard to giving. During the World Wars, the normal pattern of living was interrupted. Insecurity prevailed. Men were in service. Inflation had hit the pay check. Everybody was concerned with the immediate task of winning the war. Goods were rationed, working hours extended, transportation limited. At the end of World War II, with the discharge of servicemen and the gradual curtailment of war production, the nation began to settle back into a new sense of stability, even if it was a pseudo-stability in the light of credit buying and inflation. And with the new stability—which was really an adjustment to inflation—came a fresh plea for stability in giving, with the final emergence of the tithing movement in the twentieth century.

As the population began to rocket and as the exodus to the suburbs began to set in after World War II, the economic and social

[93] Baptist publications in the period 1920–1922 are heavy with tithing articles —cf. *The Baptist*, 1920, 1921; *Missions*, 1920; *Standard*, 1920; *Watchman—Examiner*, 1921, 1922.

climate became congenial to the stronger emphasis on tithing. Installment buying increased. Many Protestant families became more budget-minded than ever with the financing of their first home or a new and better home, new postwar appliances, cars. Living closer to the budget encouraged proportionate giving. If the American people are as materially minded as sales figures of recent years indicate, then a minimum standard in giving is certainly welcomed. It is perhaps harsh to say that tithing is the fruit of a materialistic suburbanism, but tithing, with a minimum in giving, is clearly compatible with the mid-century "suburban emphasis," or the rapid spending of one's income on material things. The Protestant Episcopal Church, which has exercised considerable restraint toward tithing, has some piercing observations concerning the "suburban emphasis." "Suburban emphasis implies accumulating or using things for conspicuous consumption; it implies 'keeping up with the Joneses' rather than doing things because of one's own need or desire; it implies self-satisfaction and blindness to how the other half lives that result from preoccupation with suburban values."[94] Close budgeting, one has to admit, whether for good or ill, is a correlative of suburban living, and as far as tithing is budgetary or proportionate in nature it is compatible with fragmentary and materialistic concepts of living.

In the periods of the greatest church-building activity, a revival of tithing appeared, whether tithing was compulsory or voluntary, secular or ecclesiastical. Solomon's temple was built following a great upsurge of the activity of the Levites (see page 32); and except for one minor prophet, Amos, prior to the fall of Israel, tithing is not mentioned outside the Levitical law until the period of reconstruction when both Nehemiah and Malachi mention it. Tithing certainly was popular in Roman Catholic history during the building of patronage chapels on the feudal estates and was very much in vogue during the reconstruction of St. Peter's at the time of the Protestant Reformation. Certainly it is interesting to note a parallel,

[94] From *Creative Choices in Life,* No. III: "Money and a Satisfying Life," p. 8, published by The National Council, Protestant Episcopal Church, 1949.

if not a relationship, in this century between the overwhelming mid-century revival in tithing as a technique in giving and the continuing expanding peaks in church-building figures.[95] Dr. Hamilcar S. Alivisatos of the University of Athens goes so far as to link the need for tithing directly to the need for the physical expansion of the church. He writes to me that "tithing *is not* practiced in our Church [Church of Greece]. The reason for this is that the Church early acquired its own property, sufficient to its needs, out of the donations and offerings of its Christian members." Apart from property acquisition and church construction, Dr. Alivisatos sees no need for tithes in the state church of Greece. It would be out of order to say that one causes the other—that church-building crusades cause a revival of tithing or that tithing emphases cause a revival of church-building and remodeling programs. But at least it can be observed historically that the visible material expansion of the church and tithing are generally, although not necessarily precisely, coincidental.

The upsetting years of the war, the greater urbanization of rural areas, and the challenge of new jobs in the North have brought greater mobility to the church. And this greater mobility has brought about a greater dispersion of tithing in the North. Both the Southern Baptist Convention and the Southern Presbyterian Church (U.S.)—traditionally strong tithing churches—have become more mobile and have crossed the historical southern and northern lines. Southern Baptists are organizing one new church every ten days in Illinois alone, as well as expanding successfully in Canada and New York City. The relocation of tithing enthusiasts among the more lethargic in tithing and the growth and success of tithing denominations in the less enthusiastic tithing areas of the North certainly are pricking northern Protestantism to view tithing with open eyes.

The ecumenical movement is helping to give tithing a new birth in the United States and around the world. One of the grand old men of the ecumenical movement—the late John R. Mott, who

[95] In 1957 a new peak of $868,000,000 was reached in new church building, representing an increase of $93,000,000 over the previous year.

was a distinguished leader of the Student Volunteer Movement before the turn of the century and who was named honorary president of the World Council of Churches at the 1954 Assembly in Evanston, lent his support to tithing. Once he said that if Americans would put their tithes on the altar of Christ, in five years the machinery would be started which would guarantee the preaching of the gospel to every person on the earth. But it is more than the sincere leadership of the World Council of Churches that musters the ecumenical movement behind tithing. There are these three aspects:

1. The historically orthodox and the theologically orthodox membership of the vital Commission on Faith and Order brings to the forefront of the theology of the council an emphasis on disciplines in the church. And when tithing is accepted as a discipline for Christians, it finds ready ground in which to take root in a new orthodoxy of an ecumenical church.

2. The World Council in its composition of 160 churches in forty-two countries and in its natural desire to attract new churches is always in danger of further compromises. Thus when tithing tends to become the *ordre du jour* in stewardship, the beckoning of conformity throws a conspicuous aura about reluctant churches. This is felt very keenly in merger discussions. The American Baptists are now emphasizing tithing very strongly. Could it be that this denomination, which failed with union gestures with the Disciples, a strong tithing denomination, and which has now entered fraternal and evangelistic relationships with the Southern Baptists, has been influenced by its big sister denomination in regard to tithing? One of the points where the merger discussion between the Presbyterian Church, U.S.A., and the Presbyterian Church, U.S., bogged down in 1955 was on the differences in attitudes regarding the tithe. "A group in the U.S. church," says a stewardship spokesman of the northern (U.S.A.) church, "made capital of the fact that our record was not as good as theirs." He points out that the fact that "their tradition in tithing is much longer than ours accounts for some of the discrepancies between the U.S. and the U.S.A.

churches in the discussion." However, the ninety-three-year-old tithing tradition of the United Presbyterian church did not prevent a proposed union of the two denominations—United and U.S.A.—which was consummated on May 28, 1958.

3. The communication between members of world bodies, such as the World Council of Churches, the Lutheran World Federation, the Baptist World Alliance, the World Presbyterian Alliance, encourages an interchange of theology and methods. Tithing is one of these methods that is being spread not only in other American- and English-speaking churches, but also in the whole world. This is illustrated by 1957 Lutheran World Federation delegate Pastor K. Ephraim Amos, secretary of the Federation of Lutheran Churches in Tanganyika, East Africa. His church, which is a large one with 105,000 members, has a non-tithing tradition. Founded by German missionaries who did not tithe in their country, the African church did not cultivate it either. But an interchange of ideas through co-operative church procedure is changing attitudes toward tithing. It came about in this way, according to Dr. Amos: "During World War II we had different missionaries from the National Lutheran Council, U.S.A., and since U.S.A. is a tithing country, they brought with them this method to our church. It has not been endorsed officially as yet, as it was thought that it would be a sort of legalism, but it is now being taught in our stewardship programs."

Last of all, in the examination of the currents which might have helped to bring tithing to the forefront in the United States in the last decade is the avocational interest of the average American. Sports, for the average adult, since baseball became popular at the start of the century, have tended more and more to be of the spectator type. TV has added to the spectator habits of the average American. Everything worth seeing—from the best in children's entertainment to theater and opera—can be seen in the living room. We are becoming increasingly sedentary. TV makes spectators of us even in programs in which we could participate as part of the audience. For instance, quiz programs have become so technical that all that the average man can do is to watch. On the panel programs where the viewer could guess along with the "experts," the answer in most cases is given ahead of time to avoid any cause for thought. The adult continues to be a spectator in the church worship and activities in our professional churches. Can it be that the loyal churchman becomes a spectator in giving as well? Does he prefer to follow the line of least resistance; namely, the acceptance of a norm or percentage in giving, which fits into the mold of most of his other specator habits? It seldom enters the mind of a Protestant to identify himself with the object of his giving, to participate personally and not anonymously in giving, any more than it occurs to him to pitch the next inning for the Giants or the Tigers. And he is no more ready to give creatively or actively than he is to engage in big-league baseball. Could it be that tithing is a spectator's sport?

More, of course, could be said to evaluate tithing in its historical perspective, for Lansdell filled two volumes and merely scratched the surface with his minutiae on the subject. Boyd admits that she covered a very broad subject in dealing merely with tithes in medieval history. Our purpose has been to touch the high-lights of the tithe in its Biblical, secular, ecclesiastical, and voluntary development. We have tried to get at the roots of today's proportionate giving. Before proceeding to constructive suggestions concerning proportionate giving, a number of questions are in order, not as a judgment against proportionate giving and its current expression, tithing, but as serious questions which should be raised and answered by serious men of the church.

1. ***Is there such a thing as a voluntary tithe?*** Until very recently tithing has been associated with the coercion of the church or state. But Protestant proponents of the tithe today say that the tithe in the twentieth century is voluntary, and not forced on anyone. Possibly this was true earlier in the century and up to the time of the Second World War, but is it true now? Whenever an idea becomes as widely accepted as tithing is, and as a standard of orthodoxy in giving, how voluntary is a man's decision to tithe? The real question is: How voluntary is orthodoxy and how voluntary is conformity? Many things influence a man's decision. But when he decides in favor of the status quo, is this voluntary?

Even as the ecumenical church councils of the fourth and fifth centuries dealt with the nature of Christ, and as the theological discussions of the first half of this century dealt with the ideas of social progress and the questions of Christian unity, a new subject is now emerging. It is stewardship. In coming into its own, the new field of stewardship emphasis (note new stewardship departments indicated on pages 22-24) brings a new conformity to the Protestant church, and in so doing a new yardstick by which to determine at least by inference whether a person is heretical or not. The yardstick is the practicing of or the failure to practice proportionate giving, and in particular, tithing.

The new pattern of orthodoxy is most obvious in developing church polity. A Southern Baptist deacon tells me that tithing is now a requirement for a person who wishes to teach in his church. While this procedure is not officially encouraged by the Southern Baptist Convention, it is likewise not discouraged on the grounds that moral and spiritual standards are necessary for determining the fitness of a teacher, and these standards can include requirements for giving. One stewardship executive in the East told me that he regarded the idea of tithing as "vicious" but that he could not fully state his position vocally; another intimated that he would be "crucified" if he took a position against tithing.

When the Free Will Baptists formed a national association in 1935, their constitutional booklet, *A Treatise of the Faith and Practices of the Original Free Will Baptists,* included a statement that "both the Old and New Scriptures teach tithing as God's financial plan for the support of his work." In 1956 this statement caused the Grand River district association in Oklahoma to burst into turmoil. One group asserted that this statement provided the basis for a ruling making tithing a requirement for ordination to the ministry in that district association. Fifteen of the churches agreed; fifteen dissented. Consequently, when the governing body of the Free Will Baptists upheld the statement of faith with the new clause on tithing, the dissenting churches were cut off from the church. Although the question was a wider one of loyalty to the treatise, nevertheless the only point of dissension, according to W. S. Mooneyham, executive secretary of the Free Will Baptists, was the point of accepting or rejecting the principle of tithing.

The pressure to conform to the tithing fad is strong socially. Says former Broadcasting and Film Commission chief of the National Council of Churches Ronald Bridges: "Fellowship and companies of tithers are on the increase among us, and the interest in tithing is growing."[96] A Memphis church boasts a "Tithers Anonymous" group; a Coral Gables, Florida, layman has organized Tithers' Incorporated—its purpose being to tithe youngsters into school in every state of the union; three Kentucky lawyers have organized a tithing corporation. Individual churches have their own tithing circles, and several denominations provide tithing cards for church members to sign to indicate they are loyal tithers. Although there is not the physical coercion of a Charlemagne or a Gregory VII or an Innocent III to impose tithing, there is an unwritten law that expects Christians to tithe or to join an unpopular minority. Can such orthodoxy then be coincidental with voluntariness?

2. ***Can there be such a thing as a Christian or a non-legal tithe?*** The tithe is a legal term. It is a regulation to follow, like a speed limit which has the sanction of the authority of the state police. Although tithing may not be obligatory, it cannot escape nomism. Giving proportionately is an appeal to a fixed standard; the principle of proportion is agreed on ahead of time and under a proposed sanction of the Scriptures binds the giver to his principle. Creative giving, on the other hand, appeals to no standard or principle in giving; rather it is a reaction or response, growing out of Christian

[96] From the tract "On Tithing" by Ronald Bridges. Distributed by the Fellowship of Tithers Among Congregational Christian Church Folk, Dr. Stanbery J. Nichols, Secretary, 56 Public Square, Medina, Ohio. Published 1949, reprinted by the Missions Council, 1956.

experience. The determinate in creative giving is not conformity to a principle but response to a person, namely, Christ. The very questions which proponents of "Christian tithing" ask betray the legalism of tithing. For instance, when a person asks "Am I a tither?" or "Do you tithe?" or "Do you give above a tenth?" or "Can I give a double tithe?" "Shall I take the tithe out of my whole check or my take-home pay?" he is asking questions that can only be answered in terms of a law or principle under sanction, regardless of what he might call his idea of tithing. Is there any way of dispelling legalism from the terminology of tithing?

3. ***Is tithing moral?*** Religion that is not moral cannot expect to be a redemptive or a spiritual religion. Immoral or sub-moral religion must shed the attributes of mercy, justice, love. Christianity is moral, for although it may be relativistic, it does not contradict the essence of a revealed ethic, such as the summation of the law[97] or the qualities of mercy and justice.[98] Tithing, to be Christian, must be moral, and it is in order, then, to ask the question of its moral acceptability.

But tithing "brings in grave problems of moral theology," says Jonathan G. Sherman, suffragan bishop of the Long Island Protestant Episcopal diocese.[99] "People of tender conscience feel it a hardship if they have small incomes. Also, it sets a low standard for the rich." Instead of requiring that each Christian begin with giving the tithe, Jesus says simply, "Unto whomsoever much is given, of him shall be much required."[100] Adds Southern Baptist Paul L. Stagg, of Front Royal, Virginia: "Even the government, recognizing the truth of Jesus' statement, has a better and fairer standard: It does not tax everyone by fixed percentage, but asks the more able to give a larger share of their income. If the old Jewish tax of a tenth is not

[97] Matthew 22: 37-40.
[98] Micah 6: 8; James 1: 27.
[99] Before the House of Bishops at the General Convention of the Protestant Episcopal Church in Honolulu, 1955.
[100] Luke 12: 48.

wholly moral, one ought to be very cautious before reading it into the spiritual imperatives of Jesus."[101]

An executive denominational editor told me about eight years ago that when he was a pastor during the economic depression of the thirties, a father who had difficulty paying for the food for his family came to him and asked, "Do you think I ought to tithe?" The pastor could not in conscience advise the man to tithe while the children remained hungry. Yet that same denomination today is asking for its members to tithe up and down the line regardless of salaries, obligations, or other contingencies.

While visiting with stewardship leaders in the South and explaining the nature of this book, one stewardship executive presented a very real question. He wondered what I would do if I were down to my last dime. Would I give a penny of it or would I give all. I would have three alternatives: (1) I could give a tithe, a penny; (2) I could do as the Hebrews did in later history and declare the dime as "corban," a gift from God which I did not need to return; (3) or, following my position literally, I could give all. The attempt was to show the bankruptcy of the idea of "total" giving. Actually, the question was raised in a misunderstanding of creative or total giving for ascetic giving, which is not creative giving. But the question showed something much more poignant than the bankruptcy of ascetic giving which the questioner had confused with creative giving. It showed not only the legalism engendered by circumventing the unwritten law to justify the law as involved in "corban" to

[101] It is the moral problem which is keeping tithing from being generally introduced in Japan, says a Lutheran layman, Yasuzumi Eto, assistant principal of a high school in Kumamoto, Japan: "In some denominations of the Japanese churches they are practicing tithing, for instance in the Seventh-day Adventist church. But we (Evangelical Lutherans) think tithing is too difficult for many Japanese to practice, because food is too expensive to do so. The average salary man spent 56% of his total income for food in 1957, although his dietary level is still low. As we don't have enough food, oil, electricity and housing, we pay so much for maintaining our living. We don't have a heater in winter. Also the tax is very high on low salaries. We cannot afford tithing." An American with a better level of prosperity and a better tax climate can afford more than the tithe. Tithing, therefore, becomes immoral for both Japan and the United States, and for opposite reasons.

which the questioner wanted me to appeal, but it showed the keen moral problem involved in tithing. Can the man who is down to the last dime be expected to give a penny of it?

The tithing protagonists are enthusiastic in saying, yes. They point to the benefit in giving while in poverty. It creates disciplines which can be useful in lifting a person out of his poverty, when poverty is primarily social and economic and not the prime result of external misfortune. Most important of all, it is said that tithing brings joy to the giver under any circumstances. The widow gave her two pennies. She was happier than all the others and she gave two pennies out of two pennies. (It could be pointed out that this giving was not proportionate giving, and since it is physically impossible to give in such a way unless one commits suicide or joins a monastic order, Jesus then was using the example figuratively and not literally.) Nevertheless the poor widow is generally the point in question when a tither touches upon the moral question in connection with tithing. The Texas *Baptist Standard* recently argued that "if this widow could tithe, anybody can. Then why does not everybody tithe?" In the October 5, 1957, issue an editorial notes that "it is easier for the poor than it is for the rich to tithe their incomes." This doubtlessly is true. For "it is easier for a camel to go through the eye of a needle, than for a rich man to enter into the kingdom of God."[102] But to make this statement, as it was made in support of tithing, is to beg seriously the question of morality in relationship to tithing. It is one thing for a poverty-stricken person, such as the poor widow, to give drastically; it is another thing for the church to expect her to do so, to give on the same principle as the rich man. It is certainly more "blessed to give"—this goes for the poor and the rich, and especially for the poor, then. But is it moral for the church to expect a hardship from the poor that is not equal to the hardship of the rich? Is there justice—not to mention love or mercy—in recommending a measuring standard that is applicable to the poor as to the rich? Even if it is moral to tithe, at the expense of one's family responsibilities, is it moral for the church

[102] Matthew 19: 24.

to expect such a tithe? The question is not with the individual, but with the church.

4. ***Is tithing creative?*** When one considers the great plateau of complacency in the Western world and the dire need for creativity within the church for the sake of its mere survival or emergence in this century, then it is apropos to scrutinize tithing for what might be creative about it. By certain secular standards, tithing is creative—at least in the sense that it brings results. But the immediate results cannot be the only criteria of creativity. A great beverage company in the United States practically had a world monopoly on the soft-drink business. By every secular criterion the company was a success. But in its success were its seeds of destruction, for from its conservatism and complacency emerged its weakness. When a small rival company began using machines for dispensing the drink instead of bottles, the idea took hold like lightning. Sales of the larger, established company dropped off and the existence of the company was threatened. The same judgment is true in church matters, such as tithing. Secular or physical success is not a sign of creativity. Creativity might have introduced the success, and tithing as long as it was novel was creative in the most basic element of creativity. But the moment tithing ceases to be novel, the moment it becomes the status quo, the disintegrating element sets in. Within tithing lie the seeds of destruction of giving, at least spiritual giving. Tithing as a part of a contemporary complacency can have wider implications and be tantamount to the downfall of a nation and its religious monuments.

There are some questions that should be asked concerning the creativity of tithing. The points of the first chapter pose some definite questions for tithing. What is its *motive*? To what extent is tithing a *response*? To what extent is tithing *free, immediate, spontaneous, personal, total, empathic*? Or if there are other words which one might suggest as describing creativity, let us list them and then compare tithing with them, and ask, "Is tithing creative?"

5. ***Where is a man's obligation?*** Is it only toward God? Not so, says Thomas Aquinas. "Each one must first of all look after himself and then after those over whom he has charge, and afterwards with what remains relieve the needs of others."[103] The Apostle Paul expected a person to minister to his own needs and the necessities of his own household.[104] The problem which the meeting of one's obligations raises for tithing is put quite directly by a dynamic, independent young leader of the 4½ million-member Negro National Baptist Convention, U.S.A., Inc. He is the Reverend C. L. Dinkins, director of education, with offices in Nashville. Looking up from a desk piled high with work, he explained: "I'm with it [tithing]. But not the literal interpretation of it. We are under obligations to God for *all* we have. And this includes meeting our obligations to our fellow men. The literal interpretation of tithing does not take into account changes in circumstances, such as sickness, taking care of children, or emergencies, nor increase in ability to give beyond the tithe. The Lord expects a person to keep his business—all his business, including his obligation to God's work—straight." Does tithing take into consideration all of a man's obligations, allowing for unforeseen circumstances, or is it a one way street, loyalty to a principle regardless of predicaments that do appear?

6. ***What influence does tithing have on the other areas of a church's ministry?*** Proportionate giving habits for the Christian encourage proportionate living habits. For example, a "personal growth covenant" of the Lay Development Program of the American Baptist Convention released in 1957 includes these disciplines (italics mine): "Read 'A Primer for Baptists' and *regularly* read *two* of the following [included here is a list of the denomination's publications]; visit and learn about *one* of the following American Baptist projects; seek to win at least *one* person to Christ and my church," and so on. So the matter of numerical proportion is not only a part of the modern idea of giving but also of the whole church. Numerical consciousness was a sin of David.[105] Is it a sin of the church today?

[103] *Summa,* Part II, Second Part, Question 32, Article 5, p. 1328.
[104] Acts 20: 34.
[105] 2 Samuel 24: 10.

Paul was not worried about numbers; he watered where others planted; and planted while others watered.[106] If giving is the heart of living, as far as the Christian is concerned, then proportionate giving is a basic factor in a philosophy of proportionate living. The way to get at the cancer of numericism and secularism in today's church is to do some rethinking on tithing.

A minister who advocates tithing often will advocate a correlative of tithing—the giving of a set proportion of a person's time each day to prayer and the development of prescribed holy habits. The Scripture saying, "By their fruits ye shall know them," is applied to those who sign "yoke" fellowship cards or spiritual life pledges, thus making evident that they will conform their prayer life to a pattern. While such disciplines are highly desirable (for even a second directly conversant with God is a second best spent), there is a great danger in becoming too specific.

The criticism which some Protestants launch against certain of their Roman Catholic friends who confess on Saturday afternoon and then get drunk on Saturday night could apply to Protestants who attempt to define and systematize individual encounters with God and then fail in the weightier matters. Tithing and other systematic proportionate procedures alleviate only momentarily the frustration of a worker or housewife who tries to achieve something numerically in order to live spiritually. And thus as with the old medieval indulgences, there is no real satisfaction. The only real spiritual satisfaction is active living as related to God *in sola gratia* (grace alone) and *in sola fide* (faith alone), and not in principle.

Have you ever had the feeling that you have not prayed enough, that you haven't read enough, that you haven't said enough, as a Christian? If we look at our Christian faith from another perspective than that of proportion, as the housewife depicted in the poem below, then the deep, never quenched anxiety of basing our faith on proportion would vanish, as well as the proportions which lead to the deep frustrating anxieties:

[106] 1 Corinthians 3: 6-9.

"She thought, when night had finally ended day,
'Dear Lord, tonight I am too tired to pray.'
And wearily she closed her eyes in sleep,
Slipping far into the shadowed deep.
Up in Heaven the dear Lord heard and smiled—
'Today she soothed a little, crying child;
She stopped her work to take old Ella Kloop
A fragrant, warming bowl of her good soup.
Her house was orderly, her garden tended,
Her children fed, their clothes all clean and mended.
Her husband, home from work, found happiness
And quiet peace in her deep gentleness.'
The dear Lord smiled again. "Too tired to pray?
Her hands have offered prayers of love all day.' "[107]

Satisfaction, an indefinable spiritual peace, is in total living, not in exaggerated disciplines.

Proportionate thinking can affect other church activities as well as the prayer life. There is the deacon in every church who has given so much time and who says he can give no more; the teacher who waits till Saturday night and says she does not believe in spending more than an hour on her lesson preparation; the seasonal church-goer who attends only on holy days or the regular member who says going to church once on Sunday is enough; enthusiastic, dynamic youth, surrounded by part-time, proportionate Christians, seeing their spiritually segmented peers, lose interest by droves as they reach their teens. Why cannot the church keep the youth? Perhaps the answer can be found in another sphere than in those of secular concepts of delinquency and inattention. It may be worth while to look into the church's concepts of giving.

7. *Just what is to be the criterion for tithing?* Below are the criteria on which tithing is recommended today by Protestants. Some denominations place more attention on the Bible, as the Southern

[107] *The War Cry,* Central Edition, Oct. 15, 1955, p. 24.

Baptists maintain they do. Some put more store in the Old Testament than others do, such as the Adventists. Others appeal more to the business technique and success angle of tithing. But invariably the following are the objective criteria on which tithing is recommended. In viewing them, however, we ought to ask which one or which combinations justify tithing, and which ones do not, and then use the acceptable criteria for a construction of a philosophy of giving invoking the direction of the Holy Spirit.

The criterion of universal law. As we have seen in the historical development of tithing and the facets of contemporary society which have revived and revised the historical tithe, there is nothing that warrants that tithing is a universal law. The symbol of ten is a convenient mathematical tool, but there is nothing to make it theologically universal. The arguments to support this Biblically are fiction as we have seen, and if they were not fiction, could Christians base their giving on what the pagans gave their gods?

The criterion of history. Unfortunately, in appealing to history, the church employs the Biblical and historical terminology of tithing for use in a different context. Tithing as it was in the past is not what tithing is today. Those who quote the documents of the early regional Frankish and German councils and the councils of the Holy Roman Empire, along with the forged documents concerning the papacy, in order to promote tithing should consider the full implications of an unenlightened gloss upon historical data. A Roman Catholic writer has some advice on tithing which handles the matter very well for Protestants, too. He says: "It is doubtful whether the Church would welcome a return to the old ways."[108]

The criterion of the Old Testament. Perhaps the most intelligent position on tithing today is held by the Seventh-day Adventists as they try to follow the Old Testament as well as the New Testament.

[108] "Obligation of Contributing to Support of Church," *Clergy Review,* Vol. 40, 1955, p. 542.

Thus tithing, in its general Levitical concept, fits into their beliefs; so does the Sabbath observance. But most Christians believe that the practices and rituals of the Old Testament do not belong in a New Testament church. This is what Peter discovered in his vision on the rooftop, what Paul discovered in his conversion, and what the whole church discovered in the controversies with the Judaizers. The old ways of the Jews were not to be allowed to dominate the Christians. Then are prooftexts from the Old Testament the basis for Christian conduct and polity today?

The criterion of King James prooftexts. Is it right to use as prooftexts verses of certain English versions of the New Testament any more than it is right to use as prooftexts verses of the Old Testament? What verse or verses in any of the translations of the New Testament has authority over the same verses in other translations? The Greek of the prooftexts—Matthew 23: 23; Luke 11: 42, as we have seen on page 43—leaves much more to be desired in the way of tithing than do the same quotations taken at face value in the King James version. If prooftexts are to be used to support tithing, then from what versions are they to come exclusively?

The criterion of the Bible. For the Protestant, the Bible is his visible authority on earth. It is the word of God. The Holy Spirit helps him to interpret it. The Scripture contains the record of God's plan and his covenants. "You search the scriptures, because you think you have eternal life; and it is they that bear witness to me; yet you refuse to come to me that you may have life."[109] Jesus was referring to the Old Testament Scriptures; they pointed the way to the Messiah and the way of life. They are valid today apart from their ritualisms and customs. Actually, the Hebrew Scriptures were never abrogated. They are a part of the whole Scripture, and the Christian can appeal to them as he can to the four Gospels, but he has to be careful how he appeals to Scripture; he must not pit one verse against another—the Old Testament against the New or the New

[109] John 5: 39, 40 (RSV).

Testament against the Old. The whole Bible is his guide. And he must remember the chronology and the progression of the Scriptures, that Jesus is the central figure of the Bible—his Incarnation and Crucifixion and Resurrection the coordinating events in it. True, Jesus does not destroy the Scriptures; he fulfills them. Can the tithing expert appeal to the whole Bible or does he find it necessary to appeal to prooftexts and minutiae that have no bearing on the larger Christian life and that can even contradict the Christian life as depicted in the whole Bible? Can we not let the whole Bible be a criterion for giving?

The criterion of the teaching of Jesus. The stewardship secretary of one of the largest denominations in the United States indicated to me that he felt that tithing was justified for no other reason than that Jesus sanctioned it. "What do you mean, 'Jesus sanctioned it'?" I asked. Again the prooftext in the New Testament, Matthew 23: 23 (Luke 11: 42) was cited, but this time with a different connotation from the one usually seen in the verse by exponents of tithing. The argument this time was not so much what Jesus said about the tithe or the situation of his usage of it; instead the main point was the fact that Jesus mentioned it. Most of the Jewish customs and observances Jesus elected not to discuss. But he did mention the tithe, which shows that it was in his thinking. Even if it is conceded that Jesus rebuked the tithers, this stewardship leader maintains that the rebuke did not abrogate the tithe for Christians. This reasoning, of course, begs the question as to just what Jesus taught about the tithe, or rather as to what he taught that had bearing on the tithe. Also, such reasoning leaves open the possibility of many other questions. If Jesus sanctioned tithing by mentioning it, did he sanctify wine consumption (as some leading brewers maintain he did), Sabbath observance, the priestly and rabbinical laws, Pharisaical regulations, fasting, and so on? Getting at Jesus' teachings is more than arguing from silence—what he did not mention—or arguing from the standpoint of sanction—what he did mention. Is it not wiser that we base our opinions on tithing on what Jesus did discuss and recommend directly—from the content of the Sermon on the Mount to his concluding discourses in the Temple and in the hills around Bethany?

The criterion of the dollar sign. Tithing works. But how, and for whom? Tithing works well for some very devout Christians. John D. Rockefeller started tithing when he was earning only $3.50 a week. William Colgate of the firm bearing his name, Heinz of the pickle industry, Hershey of Hershey Chocolates, Crowell of Quaker Oats were all well-to-do men who tithed. For others tithing was not a companion of physical success. "Many have never gotten rich in material things," says Merrill Moore, director of promotion of the Southern Baptist Convention. And of course he has the right attitude. For to expect to get rich introduces selfish and unchristian motives into tithing.

But whether tithing works for the individual or not, it works for the church. Figures do not lie. The Seventh-day Adventists, which expect all of their 44,000 "workers" to tithe, lead all other denominations in giving to the work of the denomination by three to one. When the denomination was organized in 1863, the tithe was only $8,000, as compared with $36,648,876 in 1953. This figure does not include another $23,000,000 which the Adventists gave in the same year in freewill offerings in addition to the tithes. The Cumberland Presbyterian church which saw only a gain of one dollar in per capita giving for all purposes from 1953 to 1955 saw a nine-dollar increase in one year (1955–1956) following official action endorsing the tithe. The Methodist Church and the Protestant Episcopal church—comparatively latecomers to the field of tithing—have seen phenomenal increases in giving since they began to promote tithing. There is hardly a church in the country that has suffered financially since it started tithing, but there are many budgets that have sky-rocketed to success. No wonder that Leonard Carr, National Baptist U.S.A., Inc., mission leader and pastor of the Vine Memorial Baptist church, Philadelphia, says that tithing "is the only way to finance God's program." Even the non-tithing Roman Catholics recognize the potential of tithing. Said a Catholic magazine: "If all of our

Catholic people were instructed . . . in His tithe law and trained correctly in the fulfillment of its obligations there would be no financial problem in the Catholic Church."[110] The most Catholic region in Brazil today is the region of Minas Gerais where the tithe was rigidly enforced in the seventeenth and eighteenth centuries.[111] Tithing in contemporary society often becomes "a device to get money," as Raymond M. Olson, Director of Stewardship, The Evangelical Lutheran Church, puts it. One historic peace church stated quite bluntly in a recent resolution that financial success was the criterion by which tithing was being employed: ". . . whereas the progress of our church is hampered by insufficient financial support, therefore be it resolved that the Christian Education Board conduct a stewardship campaign to enroll the members of our churches and church schools as tithers." The question here is simply, if tithing failed, would the churches continue to use it as a method of fund raising? Perhaps this criterion is more prominent in the popularity of the tithe than many want to admit.

8. ***What are the real fruits of tithing?*** For those who tithe there is something highly rewarding. There is satisfaction—a temporary easing of mundane anxieties which comes in any type of routine. Individuals in their testimonies indicate that there is a new joy never felt before. But the fruits or joys of tithing by themselves are not necessarily an endorsement of tithing as a Christian practice. The use of a rosary or the crossing of one's self and the recitation of the "*in nomine patris*" can bring satisfaction to certain individuals. Some have felt *extra gratiam et pacem* by touching a relic or the toe of a saint. Such experiences cannot be denied. But there is no reason to make these experiences normative for all Christians. Actually, some feeling of religious sanctification can be attached to an act which at the same time can be inconsistent with the life and teaching of Jesus.

But tithing has fruits other than those which have been borne

[110] *The Catholic Educational Review,* Vol. 30, Father Sloan, "Religious Education and the Tithe Law," p. 144.

[111] Manoel Cardozo, "Tithes in Colonial Minas Gerais," *Catholic Historical Review,* July, 1952.

out by individual testimonies. We have seen the contagion of tithing in its influence on other areas of the church's ministry. A fruit, or result, which cannot be avoided is the comparisons which tithing must introduce among Christians—the tither becomes just a bit better than other Christians. Especially when he wears a pin or joins a tithing fellowship, the other members of the church, including the pastor, know that he is among the elite brethren who are carrying the responsibility of paying the bills of the church.

Furthermore, if tithing by its lack of novelty, or lack of spontaneity, empathy, participation, freedom, and total involvement, is non-creative, then the fruits of tithing and proportionate giving are non-creative also. This is understandable when one considers the increase in the crime rate in the United States—9.1 per cent increase in 1957 over the previous record of the year before—and the continuation and deepening of international anxieties. If tithing is non-creative, and if Western civilization faces destruction in the foreseeable future, is it not possible that the fruits of tithing are God's judgment upon the church?

9. *Can there be disciplines without tithing?* Assuming that disciplines are necessary in the life of the church (for how can there be a visible church without some disciplines and/or sacraments such as baptism, the Lord's Supper?), what should the disciplines be in Christian giving? Particularly are disciplines needed when it comes to a person's finances, for the power of mammon is overwhelming. Disciplines are, therefore, desirable, if not mandatory. What can they be? Must tithing be the only one? Must disciplines be quantitative? Is there such a thing as qualitative disciplines—such as enhancing the prayer life, developing the consciousness of the love and mercy of God, the stirring of loyalties, acquiring the habit of placing first things first, asking a question often such as "What shall I do in this instance?" rather than "How much?" It is not necessary to mention specific disciplines and measures which the individual and the church can take at this point, for the last two chapters are given over to this qualitative discussion. But it is sufficient to raise the question here as to whether there are other disciplines in Christian giving, and the correlative question: Can there be disciplines that center in quality rather than in quantity?

10. ***What should be the starting point in Christian giving?*** Tithing is recommended on the basis that it makes a good starting point in giving. A person has to begin someplace; why not with 10 per cent? All of the above nine points would call into question tithing as a starting point. But putting them aside, let us dwell directly upon the question: What is the starting point? For Christians, should it not be with Christ? This is certainly true in the case with the unevangelized —he must accept Christ as Savior before he can enter the Christian life. Christ must be the beginning point for the Christian-to-be. But it does not end there. For the Christian who bears the name of a follower of his Savior, the beginning place continues always to be with Christ. Even in giving. The tenth or a proportion of any kind is not a Christian beginning point. Where is the beginning point in the teaching of Christ? Where was it for the Disciples? The beginning point was total dedication and total response. Not complete self-denial, for the Disciples did take sandals, a coat, a staff, a purse with them when Jesus sent them out.[112] But their giving was a total, organizing response. This total response was what Bonhoeffer was getting at in his idea of a revealed rather than a realized ethic. "After Christ has appeared, ethics can have but one purpose, namely, the achievement of participation in the reality of the fulfilled will of God. . . . The will of God, which became manifest and was fulfilled in Jesus Christ, embraces the whole of reality. One can gain access to this whole, without being torn assunder by its manifold variety, only in faith in Jesus Christ."[113] There we have the basic area for a starting point.

Tithing has been proposed as the first step for growth in giving. But must Christian growth be geared to or gauged by mathematical formulas? Of course not. Peter sums up the measuring rod, the

[112] Mark 6: 7-9.
[113] Dietrich Bonhoeffer, *Ethics*, p. 78.

source, and the nourishment for Christian growth: "Desire the sincere milk of the word," he said. For what purpose?—"that ye may grow thereby."[114] Can there not be a starting place for Christian giving without adopting a static formula—starting in such general areas as the word of God, reality, and the relationship of God to man?

Let us proceed to approach giving from new starting points, taking our stand from a scrutiny of the New Testament, existence, and theology. Perhaps it can be said of proportionate giving, as Sir Isaac Newton said on his deathbed, looking back over his life: "I seem to have been like a boy playing upon the seashore, amusing myself with a smoother pebble or a prettier shell than ordinary, while the great ocean of truth lay undiscovered before me."

[114] 1 Peter 2: 2.

3

The Case for Spontaneity

Since the selection of "spontaneity" as a key word of giving in the first chapter, we have seen the dangers of an opposite approach, proportionate giving. But is spontaneity a wise selection?

It behooves us as Christians to look for our answer first in the New Testament. Then, rather than to move into a theology of stewardship and a theology of gratitude, we shall make our way to theology from an analysis of life, or existence, as it is. Thus we shall build our case for spontaneity not on theory and on extraneous material, but on the Word of God itself through Christ Jesus and in the gamut of life and relevancy.

I

What does the New Testament say about spontaneity?

Consider the role of compassion in the New Testament.

When Jesus drew near Jerusalem from Perea in the east, he burst forth with words of compassion: "O Jerusalem, Jerusalem, which killest the prophets, and stonest them that are sent unto thee; how often would I have gathered thy children together, as a hen doth gather her brood under her wings, and ye would not!"[1]

The Savior expressed great compassion on other occasions. When Jesus crossed the Sea of Galilee and saw the Gadarene demonaic, he

[1] Luke 13: 34.

had compassion on him;[2] he had compassion on the multitudes.[3] In his great compassion for lost souls of the world, he saw in the agonizing moments of the garden God's will ahead for him.

Compassion is put into giving. Jesus said: "Give to him that asketh thee, and from him that would borrow of thee turn not thou away."[4] John says in this same vein: "Whoso hath this world's good, and seeth his brother have need, and shutteth up his bowels of compassion from him, how dwelleth the love of God in him?"[5] To respond to a person's need out of compassion is to give without premeditation from the heart. In calling for compassionate giving the New Testament is calling for spontaneous giving.

The New Testament also sets no standards, low or high, in giving. Jesus, in his great farewell discourse following the Lord's Supper, challenged his disciples never to think in terms of limits. Said Jesus: "Verily, verily, I say unto you, He that believeth on me, the works that I do shall he do also; and greater works than these shall he do; because I go unto my Father. . . ."[6] Speak of positive living! We can speak also of positive giving; and positive giving, where there is no psychological complex or external restraint, is expressed in spontaneous and confident action. "I can do all things through Christ which strengtheneth me,"[7] Paul said.

New Testament giving is free from anxiety. "Be content with such things as ye have:" the writer of Hebrews said, "for he hath said, I will never leave thee, nor forsake thee."[8] A contented person is not concerned with the right action, such as whether he is paying his tithe correctly or meeting other requirements in giving. Paul says: "I have learned, in whatsoever state I am, therewith to be content."[9] A Christian who does not worry about his giving gives spontaneously out of his spiritual contentment.

[2] Mark 5: 19.
[3] Matthew 15: 32; Mark 8: 2.
[4] Matthew 5: 42.
[5] 1 John 3: 17.
[6] John 14: 12.
[7] Philippians 4: 13.
[8] Hebrews 13: 5.
[9] Philippians 4: 11.

Conduct is a part of spontaneous giving. Jesus emphasized conduct as being more important than the act of putting a gift on the altar for God. "First be reconciled to thy brother, and then come and offer thy gift."[10] The Christian is right with his Lord and his fellow men before he brings his gift. The New Testament emphasis, then, is more on living and doing than on concern with the gift itself. And lack of concern with the gift itself encourages more spontaneity.

When Jesus instituted the Lord's Supper he illustrated his impending death and its meaning by breaking bread and saying that it represented his body which was to be given or broken for his followers. He asked his disciples to continue the ceremony of breaking bread and drinking the cup. "This do," he said, "in remembrance of me."[11] The remembering which Jesus had in mind was more than a table observance. Bodies were to be broken or given even as his body was broken. In remembrance of Jesus nothing was too great to give to him. The early Christians were willing to live for Christ, die for him, give without measure.[12] Remembrance was their talking point. Peter says: "I stir up your pure minds by way of remembrance."[13] In a continual remembrance of Christ the early Christians were stirred to enthusiastic and spontaneous action.

The remembrance of Christ determined the nature of the New Testament church. The Apostles had to choose between a well-ordered, self-contained church such as the remodeled Judaism which the Judaizers tried to force on them, or a new, spontaneous fellowship, in which the structure was peripheral and not at the heart of its life. The early history of the church, particularly that contained in Acts and in the Pauline Epistles, shows that the earliest Christians did not regard the church primarily as an organization, but as a fellowship between God through Christ and men and among men. The fellowship arose out of a response and an interrelationship of responses. Thus the thinking in terms of amounts stayed

[10] Matthew 5: 24.
[11] 1 Corinthians 11: 24.
[12] 2 Corinthians 1: 8.
[13] 2 Peter 3: 1.

at the periphery, rather than at the very center of the faith. But in every age there is the temptation to substitute the periphery, what is on the outside, for the center, the organization for the organism. Yet the early church kept in mind her Savior, responding to him, serving in his name. To argue against spontaneity is to argue against the essential nature of the church.

Nevertheless peripheral thinking—the philosophy of mixed values and organizational efficiency—tried to enter the church through many individuals (as Acts and the epistles of Paul indicate). Among the earliest and most notorious of peripheral Christians are Ananias and Sapphira. But their unresponsive and irresponsible actions failed to dim the inner light of the church. When their gifts lacked the spontaneity of response to Christ, they were struck dead.[14] The moral of the story of Ananias and Sapphira lies in a point mentioned earlier, that giving is not separate from conduct. Their gifts by themselves would not have been offensive. But the falsehoods they told contaminated the gifts. They were not conscious in their giving of the Christ who was crucified for them. Yet the story raises a more specific point than the general relationship of conduct and giving. Why did Ananias and Sapphira lie? What had they to gain? Surely they knew that they could not lie to God. But they did not seem to care about this fact. They were interested in lying to men. Their act was for the purpose of securing or maintaining a reputation.

This brings forth another aspect of New Testament giving. Giving in the New Testament is emphatically divorced from reputation. Simon the Magician wanted to preserve his reputation by giving money to receive the power of the Holy Spirit. Instead he received a rebuke from Peter, who had come to visit the newly organized church in Samaria.[15] Giving caused Christ to sacrifice reputation. Says Paul: Christ "being in the form of God, thought it not robbery to be equal with God: but made himself of no reputation, and took upon him the form of a servant, and was made in the likeness of men: and being found in fashion as a man, he humbled himself, and

[14] Acts 5.
[15] Acts 8: 20.

became obedient unto death, even the death of the cross."[16] Paul himself sacrificed his reputation when he became a Christian. He sacrificed a position in education and authority. And he knew well the price of reputation which he paid: "I count all things but loss for the excellency of the knowledge of Christ Jesus my Lord: for whom I have suffered the loss of all things, and do count them but dung, that I may win Christ."[17]

Jesus emphasized that giving must be separate from building a reputation when he warned against announcing gifts in public and when he directed that alms be in secret. In his warning against fusing the building of a reputation with the practice of giving, he suggests that "when thou doest alms, let not thy left hand know what thy right hand doeth."[18] Thus at least in regard to alms, or acts of compassion, there is no time to think of reputation, but rather there is spontaneity in giving. Alms (Greek: *eleemosyne*) means in its root form "mercy," "compassion." Thus we have the thought again that when giving is truly compassionate, according to the New Testament, it will be truly spontaneous.

To understand the place of spontaneity in the New Testament giving it is fitting to concentrate on what Christ himself said. As we have seen in discussing proportionate giving, Jesus' Palestinian habits and customs are not an adequate guide to Christian faith and practice. His teaching holds this instruction. And much can be learned about his teaching by looking at the parables which he told.

More than half of Jesus' parables deal with giving, or the use of possessions. Yet it may not be an exaggeration to say that all of the parables of Jesus have bearing on a Christian's giving and more particularly upon his giving spontaneously.

Jesus asks: "Can the children of the bridechamber mourn, as long as the bridegroom is with them? But the days will come when the bridegroom shall be taken from them, and then shall they fast."[19]

[16] Philippians 2: 6-8.
[17] Philippians 3: 8.
[18] Matthew 6: 3.
[19] Matthew 9: 15; see also Mark 2: 19; Luke 5: 34.

The conduct of the future is determined by the presence of the wedding guest. Giving also is to be done with joy, with a sense of the presence of Jesus.

"No man putteth a piece of new cloth unto an old garment"[20] or puts "new wine into old bottles."[21] If so, the cloth tears, and the bottles burst. The things ahead for the Christian are not decided by the old things. Giving also is not decided by the tradition of the Jews or of the church.

At the end of the Sermon on the Mount, Jesus tells of the rain, floods, and winds gnawing at the foundations of two newly built homes.[22] The one built upon the sayings of Jesus stood; the other, whose builder invested in old, cheap, and outdated materials, which would include the law, fell, and "great was the fall of it."

Jesus compares "the men of this generation" to children at play.[23] They play music and call on their playmates who refuse to dance. They fail to see the joy of the revelation of God through his prophets and his Son. They prefer to complain, label the Son of man as a "gluttonous man, and a winebibber," and await their own day of doom. The parable shows also the unpopularity of those who give their lives over to God.

Two men were in debt to the same moneylender, one owing ten times what the other owed.[24] The moneylender forgave both of them. "Which of these will love him most?" The one to whom is forgiven the most. Christians, relieved of the grip of sin when they invested their lives with Christ, are very thoroughly devoted to their redeemer and unconsciously out of their great devotion will give the most.

The parable of the sower speaks of the ground on which the word of God must fall if it is to grow and bear fruit or dividends;[25] when one responds to God through his Son there is a great increase

[20] Matthew 9: 16; see also Mark 2: 21; Luke 5: 36.
[21] Matthew 9: 17; see also Mark 2: 22; Luke 5: 37.
[22] Matthew 7: 24-27; Luke 6: 46-49.
[23] Matthew 11: 16-19; Luke 7: 31-35.
[24] Luke 7: 36-50.
[25] Matthew 13: 3-9, 18-23; Mark 4: 2-8, 13-20; Luke 8: 4-8, 11-15.

of activity, including giving. The parable of the tares points up some of the hazards and temptations of investing with Christ, which will be solved as the weeds are tied up and cast into the fire at the final reckoning.[26] The Kingdom of God is a very productive investment, coming to a blade and a head quickly.[27]

Things which appear little on earth, such as the Kingdom of God, can grow into great things, as illustrated by the parable of the mustard seed[28] and the leaven.[29] It is the little things that count, and nothing exceeds more in value than the Kingdom of God. The two parables show also the surety by which the Kingdom comes. The Kingdom does not grow by man's efforts, but comes spontaneously by God's own will, and this man cannot control.

This Kingdom can be found in the most out-of-the-way places. It is like one man finding a treasure hidden in a field[30] or a pearl of great price.[31] In both cases, the new discovery is worth the finder's complete investment. The novelty or spontaneity of the discovery continues. The Christian is like a householder or caretaker of a treasury who can bring "forth out of his treasure things new and old."[32] And God is always present, ready to help as a friend at midnight.[33] The participation of God through the Holy Spirit can bring spontaneity to a gift.

The Christian is like a bondservant who bids quickly his master's demand.[34] Constant service never ends. "When ye shall have done all those things which are commanded you, say, We are unprofitable servants: We have done that which was our duty to do." Luke in recording this parable of Jesus was aiming at restoring morale against the disappointments and heartaches of the rising persecutions. "Luke urged that obedience to Christ would bring certainty and joy and

[26] Matthew 13: 24-30, 36-43.
[27] Mark 4: 26-29.
[28] Matthew 13: 31, 32; Mark 4: 30-32; Luke 13: 18, 19.
[29] Matthew 13: 33; Luke 13: 20, 21.
[30] Matthew 13: 44.
[31] Matthew 13: 45, 46.
[32] Matthew 13: 51, 52.
[33] Luke 11: 5-13.
[34] Luke 17: 7-10.

ultimate security. The true disciple would find satisfaction in service, not in escape from it."[35]

Jesus speaks directly about monetary investment in several parables. The rich fool[36] built barns, trusting in things of this world, thus experiencing complete failure in his investment; the Good Samaritan[37] used his resources spontaneously, helping a person he met along the road to Jericho; the Prodigal Son[38] learned the error of material and selfish pursuits; the parables of the pounds[39] and the talents[40] warn against idleness when using monetary wealth. The Christian is to make the best use of his money for the Kingdom of God. He is like the unjust steward who was commended by his master for his new ideas and quick action.[41]

A person entering a commitment to Christ ought first to know what he is getting into. If he does not, he will be like a man who started a tower and could not finish the job[42] or like a king going to battle with insufficient troops.[43] A mere dabbling in the faith will be doomed from the start. Concluding these two colorful but brief parables, Jesus says: "So likewise, whosoever he be of you that forsaketh not all that he hath, he cannot be my disciple."[44]

When a person gives his life to Jesus, there is unspeakable joy in heaven. He is like a sheep that was lost, which when it is found causes the shepherd to rejoice;[45] he is like a lost coin that brings joy when it is found again.[46] The story of the elder brother,[47] who appeared long-faced at the return of his prodigal brother, is a strong contrast to the spontaneous joy and happiness of his

[35] Albert E. Barnett, *Understanding the Parables of Our Lord* (Chicago: Alec R. Allenson, Inc., 1954), p. 168.
[36] Luke 12: 13-21.
[37] Luke 10: 25-37.
[38] Luke 15: 11-24.
[39] Luke 19: 11-27.
[40] Matthew 25: 14-30.
[41] Luke 16: 1-13.
[42] Luke 14: 25-30.
[43] Luke 14: 31-33.
[44] Luke 14: 33.
[45] Matthew 18: 12-14; Luke 15: 1-7.
[46] Luke 15: 8-10.
[47] Luke 15: 25-32.

father over the return of the lost one. An investment with God is a great event. "It was meet that we should make merry, and be glad: for this thy brother was dead, and is alive again; and was lost, and is found."

Commitments or investments deal with the future, and it is with the future or outcome of the Christian investment or the failure to dedicate one's self to Christ and live spontaneously that at least a dozen parables deal directly. Among them some of the longest and most familiar deal with the last judgment.[48]

Wherever there is a spiritual investment, such as that which Jesus encourages in his parables, there is an easing of tension. This does not mean that the tension of the spirit in the world is lessened in regard to material things, but it does mean a lessening or elimination of metaphysical tensions. "My peace I give unto you:" Jesus said, "not as the world giveth."[49] A peaceful spirit begets peaceful action, attitudes, and living. A peaceful spiritual life is a spontaneous life. A trust in material things is never satisfying; but a spiritual commitment or investment is always satisfying, though it may be satisfaction amid persecution and amid an awesome consciousness of existence. At least there is decision over against the real shallowness of indecision, of living in a pattern. Spiritual satisfaction is the legacy of Jesus' parables: peacefulness of heart while life is wracked with tension—spontaneity, when the lessons of the parables are learned, in the midst of a troubled world.

It remained for Paul to put the teachings of Jesus into the practice of giving. On two occasions, Paul outlines explicitly his ideas, as he saw it, for Christian giving. Both of his formulas for giving

[48] Dragnet—Matthew 13: 47-50; Lazarus and the rich man—Luke 16: 19-31; the two sons—Matthew 21: 28-32; unforgiving servant—Matthew 18: 23-35; ten virgins—Matthew 25: 1-13; the wedding banquet—Matthew 22: 1-14; Luke 14: 15-24; judgment of the son of man (the sheep and the goats)—Matthew 25: 31-46; the cruel vinedressers—Matthew 21: 33-44; the importunate widow—Luke 18: 1-8; the barren fig tree—Luke 13: 1-9; laborers and the hours—Matthew 20: 1-16; the devils which return and settle in the unoccupied house—Matthew 12: 43-45; Luke 11: 24-26; the chief seats—Luke 14: 7-11; Pharisee and the Publican—Luke 18: 9-14.

[49] John 14: 27.

are explained to the Corinthians, the first in our first letter to the Corinthians, in which he repeats advice he had given and which he had seen work efficiently in Galatia.[50] His second outline for the practice of giving—and we should qualify our use of giving at this point to material possessions—is found in the second letter to the Corinthians, outlining as an ideal plan what he had seen work among the Macedonians.[51]

Now concerning the Galatian pattern of giving, Paul first of all says that the offering had a definite purpose. It was a collection or contribution for the "saints." He adds these points:

· A time was set for the collection. This may have been the first day of the week, or the first days of subsequent weeks, as the English versions imply: "Upon the first day of the week . . ." although the literal Greek, without reading Hebrew and Aramaic meanings into certain words, can mean "during [the] Sabbath's [or week's] one or first [hour, day, and so on]." The syntax denotes duration which does not necessarily mean continuation down through posterity, but can also mean during a given meeting or time, or during a given sequence of time, possibly terminated by Paul's arrival. Calvin, preferring a literal rendering of the phrase [taking "Sabbath" to be plural] translates: "On one of the Sabbaths."[52] As Paul speaks of a particular purpose for the gift, perhaps he was thinking of only one collection to be taken in the course of a meeting or a Sabbath day.

· Paul asks that "every one," or each one, take part. Nobody was excluded from the spiritual opportunity, which interestingly enough is being explained following Paul's great discourse on the nature and meaning of the resurrection in Chapter 15.

· The gift is to be determined "as God has prospered," or, literally, "laying aside what has been prospered." God gives to all people, good and evil alike, and we cannot use prosperity as a basis for

[50] 1 Corinthians 16: 1-3.

[51] 2 Corinthians 8: 1-5.

[52] John Calvin, *Commentary on the Epistles of Paul the Apostle to the Corinthians,* tr. by John Pringle (Grand Rapids, Mich.: William B. Eerdmans, 1948), p. 68.

giving. The verse is consistent with Matthew 5: 45 where it indicates that all prosperity is related to God who causeth his sun to rise on the just and the unjust. Man does not need to single out any prosperity as being peculiarly a reward of God; rather he chooses to give to God out of his own abundance; he is not giving back to God something that was loaned or specifically bestowed on Christians.

· Paul does not want to be troubled with raising the funds himself when he comes (verse 2). The giving ought to take care of itself, provided the people are genuinely concerned.

· He hopes to deliver the gift personally to the saints in Jerusalem, thus adding a sense of personality and concern to the gift, rather than sending it indirectly or anonymously.

· The word for the gift, which he is to take, is "liberality" in the King James, and simply "gift" in the RSV. The Greek for the word is the same as for "grace." Thus we know the nature of the gift expected. It is to be a "generous gift," and as far as grace or generosity is spontaneous, it too is to be spontaneous.

Paul's Galatian plan for giving, then, has these characteristics: a continued or prolonged solicitation will be discouraged; all are to take part; the gift will have a personal touch to it; the theological idea behind it is not one of owing a medieval lord, or God; the gift is simply to be generous, worthy of the way God gives, as depicted in the word "grace."

In the second plan of giving, as practiced by the Macedonian churches, Paul calls the Corinthians' attention to the grace of God and the way God gives, as recognized in the procedure of the Macedonians. "We want you to know, brethren, about the grace of God which has been shown in the churches of Macedonia."[53] The Macedonians were terribly afflicted with poverty and all kinds of suffering. Yet their abundance of joy or grace "overflowed in a wealth of liberality on their part."[54] The word for "liberality" here is one that means basically "single, simple, uncompounded." Thus the marginal notes of the King James include a second translation as "simplicity."

[53] 2 Corinthians 8: 1 (RSV).
[54] 2 Corinthians 8: 2 (RSV).

"Liberality" is a sufficient translation, but it must be remembered that it is liberality in the light of complete simplicity in character and deeds. It is observed also that they "gave . . . beyond their means, of their own free will, begging us earnestly for the favor of taking part in the relief of the saints."[55]

All of the qualities of creative giving as depicted in Chapter 1 are here: response, freedom, immediacy, spontaneity and action that is personal, total, empathic. Paul adds one further note to their giving: "first they gave themselves to the Lord."[56] Basic is the idea of commitment. It is Jesus' idea of investment. When a person's investment is complete and centered in commitment to Christ, giving is spontaneous, as was the giving of the Galatians and the Macedonians.

Keeping in mind the perspective of giving in the New Testament, we shall now turn to examine where man is, as we seek to bring the spontaneity of giving, as exemplified by the New Testament, into life. Let us look at the characteristics of man's life.[57]

II

What is life like?

Consider these characteristics of man's life.

1. *Life as creative intelligence.* "Every man knows instinctively that he is, somehow, a superior being. He knows he is superior to the land he tills, the machine he operates or the animals which are at his service."[58] Human life differs from animal life. Man's intelligence permits him to subdue the world, invade other worlds in outer space, and communicate and reflect the meaning of life. Regardless

[55] 2 Corinthians 8: 3, 4 (RSV).

[56] 2 Corinthians 8: 5 (RSV).

[57] For the reader's convenience, we are using "life" as equivalent to the philosophical meaning of existence. If a student of philosophy is perturbed by the mundane and biological meanings of life which life normally connotes, he may feel free to substitute "existence" for "life."

[58] From a statement by the Administrative Board of the National Catholic Welfare Conference, Nov. 22, 1953, with signatures which include those of Cardinals Mooney, Stritch, Spellman, and McIntyre.

of what a person's religion or philosophy is, it is generally conceded that man has a superior, creative intelligence that permits him to have dominion over the world and to press onward to new spheres of achievement.

2. ***Life as decision.*** "Choose you this day whom ye will serve,"[59] said the Hebrew conqueror Joshua to his people. He could well have said: "Choose you this moment whom ye will serve." Each moment of the day involves new choices. Whether one chooses atheism or Christ, his choice must be followed by other choices. "Every boy or girl, every man or woman constantly must make choices, whether he wants to or not, whether he is conscious of it or not."[60] To live, or exist, in the highest sense, means to decide. Life is full of life-and-death decisions—momentarily. A person's life is no greater than its weakest moment. Henri Philippe Pétain, France's great hero of World War I, with every honor of his countrymen bestowed upon him, in the Second World War played the role of a traitor. His medals stripped from him, he was sentenced to die, an order not carried out on account of his extreme old age. Pétain became no greater than his weakest decision.

Even as a chain is no stronger than its weakest link, neither is a man greater than his weakest decision. That is why the exile from the Garden occurred. No matter how noble Adam and Eve and their descendants are, man as represented by Adam and Eve cannot arise above their weakest decisions.

The immediate decision is always of the utmost importance. Jean-Paul Sartre in his play *No Exit* has Garcin in hell ask, "Can one judge a life by a single action?" A fellow sufferer in hell answers him: "One always dies too soon—or too late. And yet one's whole life is complete at that moment, with a line drawn neatly under it, ready for the summing up. You are—your life,

[59] Joshua 24: 15.
[60] "Finding and Using Your Talents," from *Creative Choices in Life,* No. I; published by The National Council, Protestant Episcopal Church, June, 1949, p. 2.

and nothing else."[61] A person does not rise above his decisions, consequently he is no more than his present, most recent decision.

3. ***Life as freedom.*** Man is born to be free. Nicolas Berdyaev, enjoying his new freedom after fleeing imprisonment in the Soviet Union and the decree that he would be shot if he ever returned, listed some of the types of slavery to which man is subjected. There is, he says, "God the Master, man the slave; the church the master, man the slave . . . the family the master, man the slave; nature the master, man the slave; object the master, man-subject the slave,"[62] and so on. Slavery awaits man on every hand; the failures of man's decision in the light of his finite, limited nature subject him constantly to one type of slavery or another. Man may not be conscious that he is a slave. And if he is conscious of the fact, he often does not know what to do about it. Nevertheless, man wills to be free, and in many small and great movements in history man's will has asserted itself against the routine of the church, the state, the machine.

4. ***Life as individual personality.*** Everything has its own individuality. "One blade of grass does not resemble another blade of grass any more than a Raphael resembles a Rembrandt."[63] Particularly is this true of human life where differences in personality distinguish one person from another. Personality is related to freedom. The chief reason for resentment in the jails and penitentiaries is not so much that a person is being punished for a crime that he did or did not commit, but that personality is being suppressed. A person can accept a certain fate, but he cannot accept a suppression of personality and retain his equilibrium. Once while visiting San Quentin in California I stood at the bottom of the

[61] Jean-Paul Sartre, *No Exit and The Flies,* English version by Stuart Gilbert (New York: Alfred A. Knopf, 1952), p. 58.

[62] Nicolas Berdyaev, *Slavery and Freedom* (New York: Charles Scribner's Sons, 1944), p. 61.

[63] Henri Bergson, *The Creative Mind* (New York: Philosophical Library, 1946), p. 122.

"cliff" of cell blocks, appalled at a tremendous sameness and anonymity. All the cells were the same. The routine was the same. The clothes were the same. The walls were the same. Grass and other live things that at least change with the seasons were almost totally absent. San Quentin is doing all it can to rebuild personality through work programs, some recreation, music participation, chaplain guidance. But the impersonalism of such institutions and their overcrowded conditions encourage disintegration of personality and thus work against rehabilitation rather than for it. Personality is the result of freedom. The less freedom a person has, the more he becomes an object instead of a person. This is true not only in prisons, but also in the church, the state, the home. Yet the presence of slavery all about a person does not mean necessarily that he must be a slave, too. "Only the free man is a personality and he is that even if the whole world should wish to enslave him."[64]

5. ***Life as an encounter.*** To be a person means that one must encounter other persons. Personality is social. It depends on others. Robinson Crusoe was not much of a person on his desolate island. He got along, fed himself, sheltered himself, survived. But it took the appearance of his man Friday to bring out the fact that he was still a person. Says Paul Tillich, "Only in the continuous encounter with other persons does the person become and remain a person."[65] The encounters of persons, who are free and treated as persons, permit a person truly to live.

6. ***Life as loyalty.*** A person's encounters are not always personal. He has many encounters. Among them are the gadgets about him, his hobbies, his possessions. But among all of his encounters, he is continually deciding or making his selection. This selection manifests itself in the development of a loyalty or loyalties. Gen-

[64] Berdyaev, *op. cit.*, p. 61.
[65] Paul Tillich, *The Courage To Be* (New Haven: Yale University Press, 1952), p. 91.

erally, loyalty is singular. When loyalty is not singular, then split personality results, accompanied by neurosis, constant indecision, dilemmas. Jesus makes it explicit that loyalty should be singular. "Ye cannot serve God and mammon,"[66] he said. A church member who has a split loyalty to God and mammon often is miserable trying to reconcile the two as compared to a person who is singularly consecrated to Christ in service, such as a deaconess or missionary or, for that matter, any person committed to a single loyalty even if it be mammon, such as a prostitute. A person finds it necessary to commit himself to something. For Miguel de Unamuno, the late Spanish thinker, "the uncommitted life . . . is unworthy of a human being;"[67] it is unworthy of existence. A person must be for something, and his loyalty will determine the direction of his life.

7. ***Life as change.*** Man is never the same one moment as he was in the previous moment. Organically, he never remains the same. The cell structure continues to change. As it has been said, a person dies a little bit each day. Spiritually, a person changes.[68] His language changes. Socially, he changes. His role in society fluctuates; his friends change, their impressions change, and his impressions of others change. Psychologically, his memory faculties and reasoning powers change. A University of Chicago Divinity School professor, Joseph Sittler, told the Lutheran World Federation meeting in Minneapolis, 1957: "We come to the conclusion that while the message of the Gospel remains the same, man is a moving target." Man is always changing. There is no immobility in life.

8. ***Life as unity.*** Although life is always in flux, the changes can never be wholly isolated. Even conversion is more than a mere "I believe," it is a commitment, a changed life, that goes beyond audible words, involving the whole life. "All real change," said

[66] Matthew 6: 24; see also verse 22—"if . . . thine eye be single, thy whole body shall be full of light."

[67] John A. Mackay, "Miguel de Unamuno," in *Christianity and the Existentialists*, ed. Carl Michalson (New York: Charles Scribner's Sons, 1956), p. 54.

[68] 1 Corinthians 3: 1, 2.

Henri Bergson, "is an indivisible change."[69] To take a moment out of one's life and say, "This is it," or, "This is the greatest moment of my life," a person either lies to himself or has gone through the motions of committing mental or spiritual suicide. For a person to live in touch with reality, or even to maintain that he is a part of it, as the Christian does, he cannot separate the moments of his life and, figuratively speaking, frame them for future admiration. This is not existence. It is death—life-death, soul-death. Life as existence, though it involves change, can never be cut up, as a piece of beef is cut into stew meat. Life, in its real sense—existence, is a unity. Says Bergson: "Movement is reality itself, and what we call immobility is a certain state of things analogous to that produced when two trains move at the same speed in the same direction, on parallel tracks." He calls the confusion of immobility with reality one of the greatest errors. "'Immobility' being the prerequisite for our action, we set it up as a reality, we make of it an absolute, and we see in movement something which is superimposed."[70]

Life as a unit is compatible with life as change. For example, changeability, and the willingness to change, are characteristics of the true church—as far as Christians believe, the heart of reality. Lutherans, with a strong doctrine of the grace and presence of Christ, believe profoundly in the mobility of the church, and also very strongly in the unity of the church in the body of Christ. Bishop Bo Giertz said at the Lutheran World Federation meeting in August, 1957: "The Word of God teaches us above all that the Church of God in matters of outward organization and methods of work never is finished." The church is a unity of mobility, a body or confederation of change.

9. ***Life as simplicity.*** Men who have found the greatest meaning in life are men who have done so by the road of simplicity. Certainly Jesus, the Savior, was a man of simplicity, possessing only one main garment at the time of his crucifixion; Buddha and Francis

[69] Bergson, *op. cit.*, p. 172.
[70] *Ibid.*, p. 169.

of Assisi renounced wealth in search of truth and meaning. In our own generation, men who have found meaning in life apart from the things that perish, such as Gandhi, chose the way of simplicity. When Gandhi died, even though he had had access to great wealth through his patrons, his sole possessions were gathered and photographed on a small part of a rug. Yet Gandhi is considered one of the greatest men of the century—on the basis of both his political and his spiritual leadership. In aesthetics—the field of art, music, drama—some of the most lasting and universalistically appealing expressions are the most simple.

Life, then, is a chain of characteristics, inextricably linked together. Life is *intelligence,* a quality which permits *decision.* A choice is only possible where there is *freedom;* freedom is not isolated from *personality;* personality implies an *encounter* with other things or persons. A person must choose a *loyalty* in the field of objects or the field of persons. Personality will develop, *change;* it grows, intensifies. Yet personality and all reality are indivisible. For who can take a knife and slice your personality or mine or God's? One can kill the body but cannot affect the invisible traits of man that live on in this life and/or in the next. And in the last analysis reality is not only *unity,* it is also *simplicity.* It is as simple as the little seed that breaks away from a tree and flutters to the ground. A schoolboy can tear the seed apart but he can never wholly understand it, for in the small and simple segments of the seed lies the mystery of life.

As we bring the two foregoing subjects of this chapter together —New Testament giving and a study of the characteristics of life— there is no clash. The spontaneity of life is not foreign to the spontaneity of New Testament giving. The themes of New Testament giving, high-lighted by compassion, are consistent with the *personal* aspect of human life. The active commitments or investments, for which Jesus asks in his parables, result from *intelligence, decision, freedom,* and *loyalty;* the spontaneous practices of the Galatians and the Macedonians reflect an *encounter,* namely, an encounter with Christ. The New Testament speaks of lives that have undergone *change* and continue to change under the movement of the Holy Spirit; it speaks of the Christian life as a part of a *unit,* namely, the body of Christ; and it speaks of *simplicity* in word and deed. New Testament living and giving, when considered with the spontaneity of human life, savor of life in its most real sense.

Let us now turn to theology, seeking for the moment a way of giving, not only drawn from the Scriptures, but also consistent with the aspects and facts of human life.

III

Who owns the world?

The question is logical enough when one is talking about giving. If we are going to give something, it is only natural to discuss who owns it. And the answer to the question of who owns the world, and all that is in it, must be God, the Creator.

Yet the question as to who owns the world is not a "Christian" question. A "Christian" question includes the Incarnate Christ. The fact that God formed the world and sustains it belongs to a theology of creation or to the realm of metaphysics. It answers a question on origins. But the answers to questions of existence and everyday living should not be the same as answers to metaphysical questions. The question, "Who owns the world?" is unchristian because it excludes existence. Let us put it another way. Salvation is an answer to a very serious question. But what is the question? Is it "Does God save?" If this is so, and the question and answer are from the standpoint of God, why does not God who created man create him as a redeemed creature? There is, of course, the Fall. But did God fail in his creation? The problems are great in this traditional approach to theology, which always leads to the absurd, as illustrated by the old medieval arguments as to how many angels can stand on the head of a pin. But perhaps then we are asking the wrong question. Let us try the question of the Philippian jailer: "What must *I* do to be saved?"[71] This is a question

[71] Acts 16: 30.

which you and I can answer. Paul and Silas answered it: "Believe on the Lord Jesus Christ, and thou shalt be saved."[72] The drama of the cross is within human existence. Except through Jesus Christ and the effectiveness of the Holy Spirit, God is still in his heaven. Of course, the Old Testament speaks of God affecting human existence; but the New Testament speaks of God in human existence through Jesus Christ. Without Christ the proper questions concerning salvation cannot even be raised, much less answered. We cannot answer such questions as "Does God save?" but we can answer questions from our own experiences, such as the fundamentalist question "Am I saved?" or the more academic "How do I experience salvation?" or "What shall I do to be saved?" The question is best answered with reference to Christ. Questions of life are difficult to answer in human terminology with reference to God, the creator, the omnipotent.

The temptation is to compress all the aspects of God into one, thus having one answer available at all times for all questions. But different questions demand different answers. Christianity is not a religion of sameness; its Savior is the "same yesterday, and today, and for ever,"[73] but Christ does not remain apart from a changing situation which is a characteristic of human life. When all questions receive the same answer, Christianity becomes full of inconsistencies —for example, "How can a God who loves us permit tornadoes?" "Why did my baby die?" and so on. The same answer, such as "God knows best," does not always work. Of course God owns the world. But when we enter a different sphere, such as existence or, if you prefer, human life, the question concerning ownership and giving must be different.

Consider the tremendous difficulties a person encounters when he asks such a question as "Who owns the world?" in the field of existence. If we emphasize the fact that God owns, intelligence is sacrificed. Men are no longer persons but slaves to a principle, or, as Berdyaev would prefer to call them, slaves to an object,

[72] Acts 16: 31.
[73] Hebrews 13: 8.

a divine architect, a divine owner. Man's decision can then have no real significance, since the chips are all in the hands of God; human freedom is totally replaced by duty or slavery to a task. There can be no vital sense of loyalty or commitment, only duty. If we speak only of God's ownership, and not man's, we are no more than automatons.

The emphasis that God is owner is a heritage of the Middle Ages. "The most notable feature of Feudalism," said Woodrow Wilson in his book *The State*, "is that sovereignty has become identified with *ownership*."[74] Sometimes in feudalism the land was leased to the peasants, giving a semblance of ownership. But when the cards were down, it was always obvious that the landlord took all. The idea of God as owner continues in Protestant theology, although the idea of privilege to do as one pleases sometimes outweighs the duty of the servant. "Calvin had accepted the order ushered in by trade and a new class, and it was to this order that his system was primarily addressed. From the beginning it was urban, commercial, and industrial and it was spread and disseminated in large degree by traders and workers. More and more it became the religion of the middle class. Where Calvinism was strongest, the spirit of capitalism was most apparent."[75] With Calvin, the idea that God was the absolute owner worked differently. It gave man indirectly new license to hoard and gain all he could. A "big fat tip" to God regularly given would satisfy a man's obligation to his God or master. With God as owner and the Christian destined for immediate eternity with God and his Christ, the working man received new confidence. And with a surety of his destiny, it was not necessary to acknowledge by action God in all of life.

The Roman Catholic church had come closer to the meaning of ownership in human existence than the Reformers, although the feudal organization of the church and church socialism made it equally difficult for the idea of man as owner to express itself.

[74] Boston: D. C. Heath and Company, 1894, p. 159.

[75] Frank Grace, *The Concept of Property in Modern Christian Thought* (Urbana: The University of Illinois Press, 1953), p. 28.

Aquinas came very close to recognizing man's natural powers of ownership: "The temporal goods which God grants us are ours as to ownership, but as to the use of them, they belong not to us alone but also to such others as we are able to succor out of what we have over and above our needs."[76]

Although man has dominion over the things of the world by the power bestowed on him in creation, his ownership of private property, according to Aquinas, stems not so much from his likeness to God, but rather from his fallen state.[77] "In an unfallen world human beings would find no necessity or reason for the exercise of the natural right of private property. This means that what we call the right of private possession of property is one of the evil consequences of the fall of man!"[78] In a world of objects and persons, in an imperfect world of which human life is a part, it is a natural right of man to own the things which he acquires.

Pope Leo XIII, in his unofficial but famous letter of 1891 on "The Condition of the Working Classes," explained that every man has by nature the right to possess property as his own. He arrives at this not only from the argument of Aquinas that the God-likeness in each man permits dominion and the fallen state necessitates acquisition and ownership, but also from the standpoint of the personality of man. With whatever man works, whatever he shapes or molds according to his liking, this he has some right to possess. In preparing or possessing an object, man lends some of his character traits. A Turkish artist, specializing in Bible art, to whom I commented that his pictures of the disciples and other Bible characters looked so unkempt, replied, "They all look like horse thieves in the Mideast." A part of his personality and attitude was reflected in his art. The way you and I wash windows or a car, decorate a house, plant a garden—all reveal certain personality traits. The objects of a man's labors are "that portion on which [he] leaves, as it were, the impress of his own personality and it cannot

[76] *Summa,* Part II, Second Part, Question 32, Article 6.
[77] *Summa,* Part II, Second Part, Question 66, Article 1.
[78] Frederic Hastings Smyth, "The Middle Ages," in Joseph F. Fletcher, ed., *Christianity and Property* (Philadelphia: The Westminster Press, 1947), p. 87.

but be just that he should possess that portion as his own, and should have a right to keep it without molestation."[79] This is one idea which the Roman Catholic church has in common with Communist theory—that which has value is that which has the stamp of man's personal labor. Thus the modern idea in the West of capital being built with the aid of interest rather than from active labor only is as foreign to Communism as it was to the churchmen of the past. Nevertheless, without attacking the later system of capital investments, the point which Aquinas and Leo make is that man because of his natural intelligence, his fallen state, and the lending of his personality to his possessions has the right to own.

But can man really own anything?

Once a month it is my custom to make a trip to the local dump yard with wastepaper, ashes, and other items. Until recently by the dump stood a quaint row of fences, shielded in summer with hollyhocks and in winter coated with snow and ice. The scene always seemed peaceful to me. But within a matter of weeks, the landscape was changed to make way for a new toll road. Farms were moved and forest areas bulldozed. I often wonder about the "owner" of such property, for, whether he likes it or not, he must under certain circumstances give way to the claims and offers of the state. This is the result of the law of "eminent domain" which goes back to Roman and pre-Roman history. Early in the Christian era, Augustine recognized the rights of the state over property. He went so far as to say that property was the creation of the state.

But the state has no right to own property for its own sake either. It derives its right from the common good of its subjects. Aquinas, as we have seen, maintained that a person has rights of ownership only in consideration of the needs of his fellow men. The right of the property was to be determined by the *use* of the property. Ambrose, fourth century theologian, expresses the responsibility

[79] From Leo's letter (*Rerum Novarum*) as quoted in Joseph Husslein's *The Christian Social Manifesto* (Milwaukee: The Bruce Publishing Co., 1931), Section 7, p. 260.

of ownership: "It is the hungry man's bread that you withhold, the naked man's cloak that you store away, the money that you bury in the earth is the price of the poor man's ransom and freedom."[80]

Therefore the gamut of ownership is invested in these powers:

1. God as creator and therefore absolute owner;
2. State (with powers of positive or civil law or as an order of creation, as Luther would put it);
3. The individual;
4. The community (the needy, and so on).

The first two types of ownership are in terms of principle, while the last two are the areas of ownership that belong to life. They are in the realm of personality, and not principle. But to remain in the realm of personality both the individual and his neighbors must be considered together. There should not be an attempt to split the two as Capitalism tends to do in its preference for the individual, and as Communism does with its preference for the social man (along with a preference for the state). Again ownership in terms of the individual and also in terms of group responsibility is in the realm of the present and therefore is the most real in respect to human life.

Man therefore can be an owner, as an individual and as an immediate member of a community; and from the standpoint not only of life but of the New Testament he is an owner. Man has to be an owner in order to invest. And as we have seen, just about everything Jesus said, particularly in all of his parables, deals with investments.

Now one might ask: "Does not making spiritual investments mean that we recognize God as owner? If the surety or the consummation of the investment is with God, then should we not begin with God?" To ask such a question fails to see the implication of an investment. To invest does not mean to give up ownership. We can make the investments that Jesus asks us to make, even total invest-

[80] Quoted by Aquinas, *Summa,* Part II, Second Part, Question 66, Article 7, p. 1480.

ment, and we can do it with a sense of hope or expectancy or joy for the future, but this does not mean that we must divest ourselves of ownership. This is the acute message for modern society. Investment for the Christian does not mean giving up, nor does it mean acquisition for the sake of self. Christian investment simply means giving, with all the characteristics of creative giving which we saw in the first chapter. Aquinas would speak of ownership in terms of *use*. There are other words that can be employed—such as "participating," "living," "existing," "serving," "ministering"—in explaining Christian ownership, but the word "stewardship" should not be one of them. We are not stewards or house managers. We are not merely at liberty in a house that belongs to a master; we are at liberty in our own houses with the terrifying implications of that liberty in terms of responsibility. We are new creatures in Christ in that we stand alone—not without Christ —but alone in the fact that we have possessions and great decisions to make.

Man as owner puts new activism, and certainly new responsibility, into giving. "Man actually has something that is his own which he can offer in the service of God: he does not merely return what is God's own gift, but makes his own offering."[81]

But if man possesses the tremendous responsibility of ownership, how does he, especially as a Christian, make his decision as to what to give and how to give? The answer is that he responds. As a music lover responds to the chords of a piano or violin, as a child responds to the affection of its mother, so does man, the intelligent, free creature, respond. His response may make him a slave, but he responds. He may respond to his own appetites and pride and become a slave of the vices; he may respond to the beckoning of luxurious objects and become a slavish, craving creature.

To what does a Christian respond? To Christ. In a sense, the Christian becomes a servant, too, or a slave (*doulos*), as Paul describes him. But Paul describes the action or response of a Christian

[81] Matthew Spinka, *Nicolas Berdyaev: Captive of Freedom* (Philadelphia: The Westminster Press, 1950), p. 162.

rather than his state. The Christian, experiencing Christ as Savior, is the freest man in the world, though his response may label him as a slave to Christ. To be a slave to Christ is to be a slave to a person, and since slavery excludes the fullest expression of personality, a Christian in a personal relationship to his redeemer is not in the strictest worldly sense a slave. "Neither the limitation nor the extension of my responsibility must be based on a principle; the only possible basis for them is the concrete call of Jesus."[82]

"Follow me," Jesus says. Once this call is answered, the Christian enters a state of spontaneity. He does not ask questions of motives, such as why he should give or, in respect to quantity, how much he should give. He has entered a new loyalty and responds out of that loyalty or commitment. The Church of the Brethren has caught this feeling in one of this denomination's newest pieces of literature, *Stewardship Education in the Local Church,* which says: "One becomes a Christian steward by *being* a steward, not by *hearing* about it, *talking* about it, or *thinking* about it." The idea is very close to what we are getting at when we say that Christians give in only one way and that is in response to God. Giving is a present response. Its expression is in being, not becoming; in living, not plotting; in doing, not talking.

There are three concluding observations concerning giving elicited by an approach through the New Testament and present reality and not by calling into play concepts that are foreign to the Christian life.

1. The starting point in giving for the Christian is not in principle, but in terms of personality, freedom, commitment. Thus we do not speak in terms of a proportion or of God as owner. With the inner depths of one's life, the conscious effort of giving begins, and ends. What the World Council of Churches said about evangelism (Section II) at the Evanston assembly, 1954, applies also to giving. "The first area of evangelism is our own inner life."[83] The

[82] Bonhoeffer, *Ethics*, p. 226.
[83] Roger L. Shinn, "Religion, Stewardship, and Social Action," in *Social Action,* Sept., 1956.

first area, as well as the starting point, in giving is the "inner life." Or as a Free Will Baptist, John Visser, of Amsterdam, Holland, puts it: "Only believers (born-again) have the privilege and responsibility in giving."

2. Gratitude, as well as ownership, is not an adequate basis for giving. The emphasis in giving out of thanksgiving has invaded the church through many current books on ethics which, though they differ, manage to find agreement in the idea that a Christian should give generously because he is thankful for what God has done for him. A theology of thanksgiving sounds good on the surface, but it does little for recognizing the strong sense of giving at the core of the Christian faith. Giving, primarily from a feeling of gratitude, brings in these problems: (1) Giving again is abstract, lost in a principle which governs giving; the precept of gratitude governs, and determines, the action; the soul is directed mechanically from without rather than from within. (2) Attention is given to motives, rather than the doing, which places Christianity within the sphere of conscience and ethics rather than independent of ethics, as Bonhoeffer prefers. Christianity is not at its best when governed by ethical decision and conscience; it is at its best when spurred by the Spirit of God, not an abstraction, but a personal and present reality which is experienced. (3) Gratitude, when it forms a conscious basis for giving, does not enhance spontaneous giving. Deliberation brings a certain sense of passivity. When one lives in response there is no period of reflection. Giving out of thanksgiving and appreciation is still within the feudalistic structure of the church. (4) Giving out of gratitude brings in the self as a basis for action. Of course, reference to the self cannot be wholly prevented in giving. But gratitude places giving on a very selfish plane. Inferred in any sense of gratitude, where there is a comparison with another person or another state of being, is the prayer of the Pharisee: "I thank God that I am not as other men are." At Thanksgiving our prayers are generally the same as that of the Pharisee: "Thank you, God, for all I have"; in other words, that I am not like some poor refugee in Europe or Hong Kong.

"I thank God for this and for that"; and as we bring gifts to God we expect his benediction, not of any special merit, but a general, "You're welcome." By recognizing that I am a little better off than my fellow men, I cannot help but rejoice in my favored position, especially if I make this spirit of thanksgiving the sole and conscious reason for giving.

Have you ever thought that some of the most selfish hymns, as well as some of the most unchristian hymns, are the great thanksgiving anthems of the church? This question is perhaps unjust, but not if we are considering the content of such hymns as a basis or as a motive for giving.

It is being taught in theological schools today that such hymns as "The Old Rugged Cross" and "Will There Be Any Stars in My Crown?" ought to be discarded because of the selfish references in them. But at least such hymns are close to reality and experience, in spite of some offensive terminology. The heart does yearn for Christ; emotion is a part of both life and faith, and these so-called "old-time" but comparatively recent hymns are at least acute in feeling and Christ-consciousness. Thanksgiving has a place in the church—a very important place. But let us not make it a motive for giving. It is one of the many responses which a Christian makes, but it need not precede his acts of giving. Thanksgiving is giving. A Christian gives out of a response to the presence of Christ—not out of a preconceived condition of gratitude.

3. Christian giving that occurs as response to Christ is spontaneous. There can also be spontaneity when one is loyal to a principle, such as God as owner, or that of giving out of gratitude. But such spontaneity is contrary to life and is a reaction rather than an immediate response to those principles, for the principles require reflection and full examination of motives. Giving, however, in response to Christ, welling out of the soul of an individual, coming from a sense of joy or urge apart from motive or calculation, is spontaneous. It is real giving—not the dullness that comes from meditating on a principle or the lethargy or carelessness from circumventing that principle. The encounter of Christian experience

produces a personal, charged response. And giving spontaneously out of a response is the only giving that is consistent with both the New Testament and human life.

IV

The desire to give spontaneously is the passion of all Christians. Yet it is difficult to do. Why?

The truth of the matter is that spontaneous giving has its problems just as proportionate giving and other giving governed by abstract principles.

What is wrong, therefore, with spontaneous giving and what can be done about it?

First, the problems:

1. ***Spontaneous giving is naïve Bible study.*** Against our highlighting of spontaneity as a characteristic of Jesus' teachings and the early church, it can be maintained by critics that the emphasis is in the wrong place. The liberal thinks that Jesus continually changed his mind. If this is so, some of the passages, such as the Sermon on the Mount, should not have the same emphasis as the ones at the end of his ministry when Jesus knew better what he was doing. This is the general position of neo-orthodoxy and the earlier nineteenth century liberals. On the other side of the fence, among certain fundamentalists, various schemes of dispensationalism and Old Testament ideas are believed to be a more adequate picture for New Testament grace and giving than the simple idea of spontaneity.

2. ***Spontaneous giving is psychologically unreal.*** People just are not made of the stuff out of which spontaneity is made. Few can reach that stage of spontaneity. They are not, as a farmer would say, like green hay stacked away in a hot barn on a summer day which combusts spontaneously. Much of the dead straw of humanity,

even the weakness of the flesh,[84] as Jesus called it, is in every man. Man needs programs, gimmicks, encouragements to respond at all, even when he is dedicated to a cause, unless, of course, the cause touches his heart and he burns out his life for it. Even so, everything cannot be left to spontaneity, as the Communist party around the world recognizes in spite of the blind enthusiasm Marxism can generate.

3. *Spontaneous giving is an oversimplification.* Professor Mary Frances Thelen, of Hollins College, Virginia, in her book *Man as Sinner in Contemporary American Realistic Theology*, brings this charge that can be applied to spontaneity in giving: "Liberal theology has frequently been accused by realism of over-simplifying the ethical problem by regarding God as love to the neglect of his justice. What also needs to be recognized is that the realists find 'God is love' too simple metaphysically as well as ethically. The liberal concentration upon the element of personality in God and within that, upon the goodness of God as person, had for its most obvious by-product the humanism which converted 'God is love' simply into 'Love is God.'"[85] Obviously when we yield the question of "Does God own the world?" in favor of the more down-to-earth question "What do I own?" or, in terms of personalism, "What can I do to help others?" we open ourselves to some of the criticism generally hurled in the direction of non-orthodox thinkers.

4. *Spontaneous giving ignores the "sin-fullness" of the Christian.* To be a Christian implies that there is a state that is non-christian or unchristian. Says Reinhold Niebuhr: "The devil is possible only in a world controlled by God and can be effective only if some of the potencies of the divine are in him. Evil, in other words, is not the absence but the corruption of good; yet it is parasitic on the good."[86] With this logic in mind, it is impossible to admit the

[84] Matthew 26: 39; Luke 22: 42.
[85] New York: King's Crown Press, 1946, p. 166.
[86] Reinhold Niebuhr, *An Interpretation of Christian Ethics* (New York: Harper and Brothers, 1935), p. 73.

complete sanctification of the Christian, as certain Wesleyan and Holiness groups maintain; it also throws a wet blanket on any type of liberalism, such as social progress and betterment of the world, and on creative approaches to problems such as the approach of this book. A creative approach is always more optimistic than an orthodox one; creative theology is always interested in new things and looks for the positive in human life; and it is not marked by quirks of reasoning or complacency. Nevertheless, the pessimism of modern orthodoxy remains a true picture of man—especially in the light of two world wars and the advent of the nuclear and space age.

5. ***Spontaneous giving fails to realize that definite disciplines are necessary in the Christian life.*** Man by himself cannot be trusted. You and I cannot be trusted to gain and dispose of wealth by ourselves any more than a dictator can handle the matters of the state. We need checks and balances as well as the branches of government do. Secondly, it is said that we need disciplines, for the most effective and sacrificial giving comes not out of unbridled spontaneity but out of the direction of the church and the regular holy habits of the individual. "Self-discipline brings self-denial";[87] it is not self-denial that brings self-discipline. To give creatively at all, then, it is argued, one must conform to certain rules or patterns; otherwise the sinfulness of man, even of the redeemed creature, will keep him from the task of his calling and the practice of giving spontaneously. Man needs checks and balances and goals and rewards—it is all a part of his nature, a part of the game. By setting definite goals and proportions in giving, "suddenly the Christian discovers it is more blessed to give than to receive."

"The notion that complete understanding controls the actions of men is a cloudlike ideal at variance with practical life. Without

[87] From the tract *Afraid to Pledge?* by Emil Krause, produced by the Lutheran Laymen's Movement for Stewardship of the United Lutheran Church in America, 1957.

routine, civilization vanishes."[88] Disciplines are needed to keep all of us, as absent-minded professors by nature, on the sidewalk of life.

6. ***What actually happens when giving is spontaneous?*** By *The Christian Century* this is called the author's "most vulnerable point." A statement by Methodist pastor Wayne W. Woodward, Shoals Circuit, North Carolina, amplifies this viewpoint. Says Mr. Woodward: "The idea of spontaneity in giving is good, but in the average church with the average Christian such a system of giving will result, I am afraid, in more and unproportionate giving to dramatic and specifically interesting causes; while the real need is full support of the rather undramatic day-by-day work of the church."[89]

7. ***The spontaneous giver is prejudiced.*** He is prejudiced against all existent corporations, traditions. His giving is like the radicalism which Bonhoeffer describes: "Radicalism always springs from a conscious or unconscious hatred of what is established."[90] Concerned with the ideal, radicalism is always looking toward something that is perfect, even though it knows that its goal can never be realized in time. Its eyes are on the eternal or on what there is of the eternal within time. "Radicalism hates time," says Bonhoeffer. This applies to Christian spontaneity, where Jesus has entered time and conquered time; it applies to the radicalism of Communism where a utopia is expected to evolve out of a class struggle. But the alternative—a compromise or acceptance of what is here—is no better. "Compromise hates eternity," Bonhoeffer says. "Radicalism hates patience, and compromise hates decision. Radicalism hates wisdom, and compromise hates simplicity. Radicalism hates moderation and

[88] "Is Anti-Tithing Un-Christian?" *The Christian Century*, March 13, 1957, p. 319. Editorial was prepared in answer to correspondence received on the author's "Is Tithing Christian?" Feb. 13, 1957.
[89] *The Christian Century*, March 13, 1957, p. 320.
[90] Bonhoeffer, *op. cit.*, p. 87.

measure, and compromise hates the immeasurable. Radicalism hates the real, and compromise hates the word."[91]

There we have the dilemma spontaneity creates for the Christian —it is something he should follow, or a way he should live every day; but though he is forgiven his sins, he is still a finite creature, a "poor sinner," as Luther says in his shorter catechism, and cannot be expected to live like a god. It is this truth, or rather the allowance for the possible verification of the criticism of spontaneous giving on the grounds that man is a sinner, that we want to recognize as we proceed to talk about creative giving in practice.

But to avoid any suggestion that the author is ready to renounce his case for spontaneity at the first injection of criticism, let us face the above criticisms.

Concerning the charge that "spontaneous" giving is naïve Bible study, we shall leave the matter with the opponents to present their case from a Biblical point of view, to isolate the sections of the Bible they want to follow and with this procedure show how they will bring proportionate giving from fiction into the Bible, the legalism of the Jews into Christianity, and Christianity into the legalism of the Jews.

Concerning the psychological make-up of the individual, we maintain that there is or should be a difference between the unregenerate and the generate. The reasons for this naïve position we prefer not to argue formally, but rest the case with the fiery testimony of the man from Tarsus, whom Christ delivered from a great weight of sin, and with the many "saints" who followed him.

To the charge of oversimplification in theology we again plead guilty. We have neglected seriously, but not discarded, the righteousness and justice of God. We have given more consideration to a "God of love." But the reason for this is not to build a utopia on earth, but to recognize God in his most fundamental relationship to man, through his love and his crucified Son. A God of justice has little relevance in human life. This does not deny that God

[91] *Ibid.*, pp. 88, 89.

is just. But if the current civilization is to get anywhere, endure and survive, it cannot do so under the thesis that God is just. There is too much suffering in the world to talk about a God that is good and just. Says Berdyaev: "No world order can be reconciled with unmerited suffering, even if it be of only one creature, with one tear of a tortured child."[92] Evgueny Lampert, in a commentary on Berdyaev's thought, says that "God does not explain or justify the anguish of life, but takes it on himself, and tastes its full horror, and in so doing illuminates it."[93] This we can accept, whether we understand it or not. God has entered existence. But God has done so as a God of love, and not as a just God. Here theology must take roots if it is to have any meaning at all.

It would be folly to deny that man is a sinner, that even after he experiences salvation he is wholly free from selfish desire. The most altruistic men in the world can be the most selfish. Donald Walhout in the quarterly *Theology Today* tells of a leading citizen in the Midwest who devoted his life to giving to others. He even became president of a local charity dedicated to stamping out a certain disease. But when he acquired the same disease and was offered help by his own charity, he committed suicide. He had learned to give, but he had not learned to receive.[94] There was still the hidden element of pride and resentment which had been building up over the years. We recognize that this sense of pride is in every man. But does recognizing that man is a sinner mean that spontaneity in giving should be de-emphasized? Or does the fact that man is proud and is a sinner mean the opposite—that there is even more reason to emphasize spontaneity? Because man is a sinner does not mean that we should throw up our hands in despair. Perhaps if spontaneity is the result of a commitment to Christ and the fruit of the Spirit, more ought to be said about the commitment to Christ and the spontaneity of a relationship to him and less about

[92] Berdyaev, *Slavery and Freedom*, p. 86.

[93] Evgueny Lampert, "Nicolas Berdyaev," in Donald Attwater's *Modern Christian Revolutionaries* (New York: The Devin-Adair Co., 1947), p. 350.

[94] Donald Walhout, "Deeper Levels of Christian Ethics," *Theology Today*, July, 1957, pp. 172-3.

the interpolation of what should come between the commitment and the fruit of the Spirit.

We have already conceded the fact that disciplines are necessary in the Christian life; our only question is, and still remains: Must we say that disciplines are quantitative? It will be our burden of proof in the next chapter to show some concrete steps which can be taken to encourage giving that will be spontaneous. As to the question whether routine is necessary for preservation of a civilization, we would add the injunction of Chapter I that creativity, and not routine, is necessary, if not the most important long-range need for the survival of civilization.

To the critics who say that the churches would suffer financially if giving were entirely spontaneous, we recognize this possibility. But we recognize also that churches can be very successful with virtually no trace of external coercion or disciplines in giving.[95] We merely recognize the basic trait of the church—that it is an organism and not an organization. If Christ be the head, the members of his body need not worry or resort to any questionable means for raising funds. We know that proportionate giving is good business. But to this point we add one question: Is good business Christianity?

Again we must agree that a spontaneous giver is prejudiced—against traditions, against institutions, against the things that are passé, and that please most anyone. Perhaps this is the spontaneous giver's great sin. Yet if it be a sin, then what shall we say about the extreme prejudice of Amos and the other prophets against the institutions of their day and Jesus' unrelenting attack against the Pharisees and their company? The religious man always lives

[95] For example, according to a Nashville pastor and author, Batsell Barrett Baxter: "Very few of the congregations of the Churches of Christ have any kind of pledge system. Ninety-nine per cent simply have a free-will offering on the 'first day of the week.' The church that I serve has 1100 members, and no one knows what any other member gives. We have no pledge system, no keeping of records on individuals, nothing but the counting of the money in the baskets each Sunday morning. We seldom preach on the responsibility of giving—I don't recall having done so last year—but our contribution was $2400 per Sunday, a total of $125,000 for the year."

as if there were something more to his life than what he finds waiting for him. He is out of place in time, but not necessarily blind or visionary. Surely anachronism is not a sin and does not necessarily indicate an error of judgment.

Now that we have made our case for spontaneity, as well as a brief answer to the critics of spontaneity in giving, we shall concede them the floor, realizing that there must be an element of truth in the saying that man is not perfect and cannot become perfect in this life, even though Jesus' ideas seem to have been different on the subject in certain instances.[96]

By seeking an application of the thesis of this book in light of its criticism, we take not only the most realistic approach to the subject, but also the most creative. For creativity does not consist of pushing on full-speed ahead. True creativity must at all times take into consideration its opposites, not discarding them, but bringing them together with the main thesis. True creativity is always a synthesis. This is the classical idea of creativity. Says John Macmurray: "For instance, in the Dialogues of Socrates or Plato there is often the statement of a positive thesis of a truth, or partial truth. A challenging antithesis brings out the inadequacies of the partial thesis. Instead of a debate to try to prove one individual or position right or wrong, the discussion ideally should end in a synthesis which should combine the values of partial truths of both."[97] With him agrees a current spokesman on creativity in the secular field, Alexander Osborn of Batten, Barton, Durstine and Osborn, Inc.: "Synthesis is generally regarded as the essence of creativity."[98]

How can we then reconcile spontaneous giving with the cold fact that man is an imperfect creature of nature? As we keep the thesis of spontaneity, we shall look for ways by which spontaneity can be strengthened on the cold, hard bedrock of life.

[96] Matthew 5: 48; 16: 17-19; Mark 9: 23; John 14: 13.

[97] John Macmurray, *Creative Society* (New York: Association Press, 1936), p. 9.

[98] Alexander Osborn, *Applied Imagination* (New York: Charles Scribner's Sons, 1953), p. 280.

The issue shall be, as a writer in R. M. MacIver's symposium *Integrity and Compromise,* puts it, "not how to live in a world free of compromise, but how in the dilemmas of an imperfect world to choose what is in the direction of perfection."[99]

[99] Eugene Exman, in *Integrity and Compromise,* edited by R. M. MacIver (New York: Harper and Brothers, 1957), Chap. 10, "What Is the Right Thing?" p. 105.

4

Churches Face the Problem

There are ways in which the churches can encourage creative giving. And since we prefer not to speak directly of ideal, spontaneous giving, which leans to the impractical, we shall speak of more down-to-earth, creative ways of giving, of which spontaneity is a part.

What are some of the things the churches can do to spur creative giving?

Use the laymen

The use of the layman in as much activity of the church as possible encourages spontaneity in two regards: (1) the more the layman is used, the less is the demand for a professional staff, which cuts down the operating budget and consequently the necessity for soliciting funds; (2) the layman becomes more personally identified with Christ in the work of his church and therefore is in more of a position to respond.

A lay ministry was important in the early church and was one of the reasons that encouraged spontaneous giving. There was not a special clergy set aside like the Jewish hierarchy that depended on tithes. Paul's silence on the tithe and his emphasis on spontaneity go hand in hand and perhaps stem from his concept of the ministry. "I have coveted no man's silver, or gold, or apparel. Yea, ye yourselves know, that these hands have ministered unto my necessities, and to them that were with me."[1] Paul again says that he preaches without charge;[2] on another occasion he speaks of an occupation of making tents.[3]

Some churches carry this emphasis on a lay ministry in the New Testament over today—some more literally than others. The Plymouth Brethren, for instance, run their church meetings without a professional clergy. Other denominations, such as the nine-million-member Methodist Church, permit laymen to preach and conduct church services. Baptist churches give laymen an active part in the holy ordinances of the church, such as the administering of the Lord's Supper. The Lutheran Laymen's Movement of the two-million-member United Lutheran Church pioneered work in church giving as far back as 1907 and organized in 1945 a department of stewardship which is supported by laymen outside the budget of the church.

To get laymen to work in the church, the church will need to alleviate the fears of laymen stemming primarily from lack of training and bad placement.

How can the church train laymen?

In Philadelphia recently Elton Trueblood presented before the American Baptist Convention a plea for seminaries for laymen. He suggested that training similar to the training for ministers could be given the laymen. This is what the Luther Theological Seminary of St. Paul, Minnesota, did during the summer of 1957 by enrolling college and nursing-school graduates only. The subjects were Biblical and theological, and were conducted on a graduate level.

Have faith in the laymen. Use them—in the pulpit, and even at the altar rail. Do not underestimate them. What the church needs

[1] Acts 20: 33, 34.
[2] 1 Corinthians 9: 18.
[3] Acts 18: 3.

is not more technicians, as some people lead us to believe, but more laymen without complexes, challenged and willing to work in the church.

Employ plans that are creative

For a church to encourage creative giving, its methods need to be creative. And the churches have a creative plan in the popular Every Member Canvass. Basically, the plan seeks to put pledge cards in the hands of every member of the congregation by personal contact. Laymen are enlisted to call on members of the congregation. By going into the homes, the canvassers confront each member directly with the task of the church and the importance of his own giving in that program. The most creative aspect of the plan is the freshness it gives to giving. Laymen are utilized, thus bringing them actively into the fellowship and tasks of the church; the people who are reached are contacted personally rather than by letter or phone. People are treated as persons, a basic condition for eliciting creative action.

The personal element is being high-lighted still further by changing the name of the canvass. Thus the Evangelical Lutherans prefer to speak of the Every Member *Visit,* rather than "canvass"; also the Maritime United Baptist Convention of Canada speaks of the Every *Person* Canvass. The Church of the Brethren speaks of its canvassers as "missioners," thus retaining the purpose of the visit and the urgency of the Gospel in the wording.

In the United States tithing often is linked with the Every Member Canvass. But this is not necessary for the success of the canvass. The Lutheran Free Church saw an eleven-dollar increase in giving per confirmed member for all purposes in 1955 while using the EMC emphasis and at the same time refusing to talk up tithing. A Congregational minister who visited the United States in 1954 has brought the EMC into Australia, but apart from the tithe. "Tithing is not practiced by Collins Street Independent Church, or indeed, by any Congregational Church in the Commonwealth of Australia or the Dominion of New Zealand, to my knowledge," says Pastor Lyall Dixon. Nevertheless, he notes that the Every Member Canvass, or Every *Person* Canvass, as he calls it, "is beginning to revolutionize the whole of our church life; the spiritual stimulus which has come as a result is indeed very marked even now." Thus it is possible to separate the non-creative—the static, impersonal elements of giving, such as tithing—from the creative, personal, and spontaneous aspects of giving.

A variation of the EMC is the Sector project originated by the American Baptist Convention about ten years ago under the supervision of a fund-raising firm, Marts and Lundy.

The main characteristic of the Sector idea is the bringing together of local leaders into one central location for training—this permits closer and more thorough preparation in canvassing techniques and the use of special materials, as well as providing the essential inspiration and motivation. This idea of training the leadership of a certain area or sector at once rather than dealing directly and immediately with the local church is responsible for the name of the Sector project.

Today this gathering of leaders of several churches at one central location is the essentially new element of the Sector project and it has had its result in better equipping the leaders of the local canvasses. The advent of the Sector approach has introduced a number of new ideas and procedures into the Every Member Canvass itself. Among these are (1) a wider and more coordinated use of charts, (2) the examination of the church program at the outset (this includes the answering of a series of questions by the church lay leaders under the general category of "What could my church do if it were really in earnest?"), (3) the use of an appraisal committee (also called evaluation or resource committee) which answers certain questions about each member of the congregation. Questions the appraisal or evaluation committee members ask themselves as they work alone in the single meeting are: (*a*) Would Mr. Jones make a good leader? (*b*) Would he make a good worker? (*c*) What would he give if he were really interested in the church?

This information about Mr. Jones and his fellow church members is put in the hands of the team of canvassers who call upon them. Although the potential donor, such as Mr. Jones, is not supposed to see the information in the hands of the team callers, unless he requests it, Mr. Jones knows that he has been "sized-up," and he is generally more willing to cooperate than to make excuses.

It is at this point of appraising one's neighbors that the Sector plan has come under criticism. A Congregational-Christian executive expressed these two objections to me: There is a tendency to pick out the top ten givers and give them preference; second, the appraisals are contradictory to the spiritual nature of giving.

The Every Member Canvass and the Sector project that prepares canvass leaders more thoroughly are creative techniques, but great care should be taken that the personal approach and the spiritual enlistment qualities of these canvasses are not eclipsed by ulterior motives and secular fund-raising machinery. There is some feeling that the term "Sector" is not the most evangelical and Christian word that can be used. In January, 1958, fifty United Lutheran Church leaders who met in New York City to study stewardship procedures gave particular attention to replacing "Sector" with another word, but did not announce any definite decision at that time. Doubtlessly the name will be changed in the future by most of the denominations using this approach; and it is the hope of the author that as the terminology approaches the content of the gospel, the gimmicks and procedures adopted in the various aspects of the canvasses will likewise continue to move in the same direction rather than in a secular direction.

Let spontaneity create the budget

Before the EMC is launched by the local church, the finance committee of the church usually prepares a budget. Definite figures and goals are then presented to the members of the church. The members subscribe to the program, pay the bills, and the church continues with a budget relatively the same as that of the previous year.

But there is a more reckless plan, that is, not planning the budget until after the canvass. From the results of the Every Member Canvass, the finance committee knows how much the church will have for spending, and it suggests a budget which will not be a guide to giving of the congregation but a guide to spending. To the businessman the plan without any set amount as a goal appears risky; but spontaneity and the working of the Holy Spirit can be effective, too.[4] Consider testimonies of two Presbyterian churches using the spontaneous approach. From a small (115-member) North Carolina church comes this result of pre-budget canvassing: "Giving in our church is on a much higher spiritual level than at any time in our history. This year our pledges doubled over last year." From a large (1,070-member) West Virginia church: "It was the most deeply spiritual canvass we have had. It removed the financial program of the church from a purely monetary basis. . . . The total amount pledged by individuals was 27% more than was pledged by individuals the preceding year."[5] Spontaneity is not too idealistic when it comes to planning the budget.

The spontaneous methods of attacking problems in industry could be applied to the problems of determining a budget in a church. Brainstorming, for example, can fire new enthusiasm and instill high goals in a church's giving. By taking a problem such as "What can our church do in the community this year, or on the mission field?" a small or a large group of representatives of the church can list one idea after another as to what can be done. Soon the list becomes fabulous. A rule of brainstorming is that no idea is too ridiculous or too impossible. In fact, there is no such thing as a negative idea. Only after several hundred ideas are collected are the workable ones sifted out. But this sifting can be revolutionary

[4] This is John Wesley's thesis on giving. In a letter "To a Member of the Society," Feb. 7, 1776, he says: "In this [approach to giving], it seems, we must needs be directed from time to time, by the unction of the Holy One."

[5] From "The 'Pre-Budget' Canvass—A More Excellent Way," prepared by the General Council, Presbyterian Church, U.S., Atlanta, Ga.

in church planning. New vistas will be seen; new opportunities for service will be recognized, and the ideas will have come from the individuals themselves.

Brainstorming is not new to the church. It has been seen in discussion groups under such titles as "buzz-sessions," "Phillips 66 plan," "sharathon," "cell groups." Imaginative program planning is the result of such sessions. Perhaps imaginative budgets could also be the results of such spontaneous techniques when churches view their role of responsibility and redemption in the community through the spontaneous approaches of group dynamics.

Encourage projects

Becoming identified with a cause is necessary before giving is accomplished. It is true with both God and man. God had to be identified with the cause of man before he could really give, that is, send his only Son to be incarnate in the flesh. Christians are identified with a cause also—the cause of Christ, the cause for which he died. They are actively seeking to win the world as he did. When a Christian's loyalty to Christ is translated into life, he becomes identified with a number of constituent causes. We can call these projects, or things that Christians can do—definite places where he feels that he can pitch in.

If Christians can identify themselves directly with the causes of their church, they respond more willingly from the heart. And there is no better way for the church to encourage the feeling of indentity than by stirring up interest in specific projects of the church, not for the sake of the project itself, but for the sake of other persons for whom Christ died.

Projects can vary from painting a Sunday-school room to raising livestock on a farm. Consider the creative aspects of this project of a Midwest rural church: Forty calves were bought for $3,200. These calves were raised alongside the other cattle on the farms of the parishioners. When the calves were finally sold, the church realized more than $2,200 profit. Such a project is creative not only in its novelty and simplicity but (1) in the spontaneous response it elicited day by day as the men took care of the animals and (2) the totality of the response in that all their resources were employed in the realization of the project.

In getting a project under way, Ralph Shrader in a booklet put out by the Missions Council of the Congregational-Christian churches suggests that "the local church committee on missionary education and promotion (or a committee with the same purpose by whatever name) meet with the minister to consider the advantages of a personal approach to our Christian work at home and abroad through doctors, nurses, teachers, ministers, student workers, schools, hospitals, churches, or various other work. The personal approach results from adopting some person or unit of work as a project."[6] Bishop Bo Giertz of the Church of Sweden describes the weekly offerings in the Church of Sweden (in addition to the church tax): "Every Sunday there is an offering for special purposes (mission, a deaconess home, the Sunday school, the high schools of the church—every Sunday a *different* item). The weekly offerings vary. A member might give a quarter to something he knows very little about, and 100 crowns to the mission on the next Sunday." People give more spontaneously and creatively when anonymity is eliminated.

Decentralize organization for handling funds

The personal element can be preserved in giving by the way that funds are handled. The closer to home the decision concerning spending is, the more personal it is, and the more enthusiasm and creativity will be engendered on the part of each member involved in giving. While some denominations send their money which is over and above the local expense to their denominational headquarters, which in turn directs the money back to the areas or state associations and various causes of the denomination, the Southern

[6] From "Envelope Series," Stewardship Issue, Summer, 1956, pp. 13, 14, issued by The Missions Council of Congregational-Christian Churches, James E. Waery, editor.

Baptists approach the dispersal of funds in a different way. The state convention, and not the national denominational boards, divides the money and says where it will go. "This builds a more effective organization," a Southern Baptist executive says. However, the national executive committee does set the percentages of total income to the cooperative program that will be apportioned to each agency and board. In the last analysis the executive committee decides who gets what and how much they will get. Although the Southern Baptist Convention is often accused of hierarchical tendencies in many areas of its life, a creative facet of its finance program is in its decentralization, or appearance of decentralization.

Enhance the encounter

Some churches rely on tricks and gimmicks to bring money into the church; yet a spiritual church program need not depend on gimmicks. It will be concerned with the spiritual climate in which the giving occurs. As long as the breath of the Spirit of God is the breath of the church, the giving is no problem. "Without a doubt our greatest progress, judging from persons received by profession of faith," says R. R. Hodges, assistant to the general secretary of the Nazarene Church, "comes at a time of spiritual revival. Our increase in giving correlates with this, also."

The key to creative, spiritual giving lies in increasing the piety and devotion of the congregation. The Protestant Episcopal Church has been quick to recognize the need for this emphasis in training its laymen. This denomination has been putting on a series of local "parish life conferences" across the nation, averaging more than two hundred a year. This has been done very quietly and unassumingly. (Attendance of the press is generally refused; however, the author was able to cover a parish-life conference in Racine, Wisconsin, for a magazine on the arrangement that another reporter accompany him.) A parish-life conference is made up of about a dozen people, usually five or six couples and a leader, attending a concentrated two-day retreat (fifteen hours a day) in which all the time is directed toward (1) worship and (2) recognizing through a series of role-playing techniques the basic need of the individual for Christ. The need is translated into life by discouraging activities of the church that are not basically spiritual in nature. A week end of such intense concentration leaves one deeply renewed in faith. By making a person fully conscious of his relationship to God and his redeemer, Jesus Christ, such a method as this which enhances the relationship opens the door to giving that comes from the heart. It is encouraging to note that The Methodist Church is interested in organizing similar conferences and also that the Disciples of Christ launched two spiritual-life conferences in 1957 for the first time.

Confession should be the heart of every church. "The free confession of guilt . . . is the emergence of the form of Jesus Christ in the Church. Either the Church must willingly undergo this transformation, or else she must cease to be the Church of Christ."[7] Those who learn to confess learn also to give creatively. Baptist and other denominations which almost completely ignore confession in any form might well study the place of the confession in Lutheran churches. Giving in the light of confession and the forgiving grace of Christ might bring more spontaneity to the "free" churches even as there is more spontaneity and less restraint in giving in the Lutheran churches, which are the greatest if not the only real restrictive force on tithing today. Churches that enhance the encounter greatly enhance creative giving.

Educate the youth

Since a person's habits and outlook on life are formed early, it is important that his ideas of Christian giving should be properly cultivated as early as possible. Is the church training its young people to give to Christian work? According to the Gilbert Youth Survey in the fall of 1957, 16,000,000 teen agers had an income of

[7] Bonhoeffer, *Ethics*, p. 51.

more than $531 a year—four times the figure for 1945. The chief purchases of these young people were cars, phonograph records, fountain pens, and clothes. The only goal for 25 per cent of them was car ownership. In a special survey of girls, contributions to church and charity were listed by 5 per cent of girls 11 to 13, and by 2 per cent of girls 14 to 16.

These steps can help to develop spontaneous and creative givers who will grow to be more effective members of their church and society:

Throw out the word "stewardship." Experienced church leaders across the country agree that "stewardship" is problematic for children. Lindley M. Franklin, Jr., assistant treasurer of the Protestant Episcopal Church, says that "stewardship is not readily understood as a word." A study book of the Church of the Brethren entitled *Stewardship for Juniors* states that "stewardship as a concept in the abstract is too difficult for children to understand." Roland S. Fredericks, secretary of Youth Stewardship of the Presbyterian Church, U.S.A., says, "we have a great many problems with the word stewardship. As a word it is difficult for young children to understand. Its derivatives as used in the secular world are quite removed from the Biblical meaning: for example, the word 'stewardess.'" This is the word with which the denominations are trying to communicate the idea of Christian giving to the children. It is not only very bad theologically, but it is uncommunicable. Cannot the church use another word at least for children? How about such active words as "ambassadors," "soldiers," "commandos," "disciples," "messengers," "couriers," "missioners," "givers"? The Joint Department of Stewardship and Benevolence of the National Council of Churches in suggesting themes for the Every Member Canvass campaigns has not hesitated to use simpler words for adults. The 1957-1958 theme is "To Give Is To Live." It could have read "To Be a Steward Is To Live," or "Stewardship Is Life," but it does not. It is effectively simple. Can we not talk simply also to our children?

We must, if we really want them to understand what it means to give creatively.

High-light the virtues of creative giving. Virtues to be translated into boys' and girls' terms include simplicity, freedom, patience, commitment, personal concern for others. "The practice of an additional group of cardinal virtues needs to be preached—simplicity, economy, self-control. These qualities should be the theme of frequent sermons, of Sunday-school lessons, of classes for catechumens and enquirers, and should be made synonymous with the Christian life."[8]

Creative worship services encourage creative giving. American Baptists are training their teachers of juniors to use fifteen minutes of each Sunday-school hour in leading their pupils to plan and put on a brief service of worship. The pupils select their own Scripture and songs, make up their own prayers, take the offering. This creative, spontaneous participation cuts down passivity in worship. Each child has a part, and by being drawn consciously closer to God he sees the meaning of the gift and enters more fully the giving relationship between God and man, namely, in commitment to Christ.

Present true stories of sacrifice. Stories from the Bible can range from Abraham, giving up his best to Lot, through the New Testament and the persecution suffered joyously by the early Christians.[9] The application part of the curriculum can be weighted with stories ranging from the early martyrs to present-day athletes who make sacrifices or have made sacrifices for God (for example, Johnnie Lawrence of England, cricket star, who suffered financially by refusing to play on Sunday and who refused to take part in the traditional raffling, or Dave Burnham of Akron, Ohio, who turned down a number of offers to play professional football so that he

[8] J. Merle Davis, *Mission Financial Policies* (London: International Missionary Council, 1945), p. 93.

[9] Acts 12, 16; 1 Peter 3: 13-17.

could serve God fulltime). "Young people need to be reminded that sacrifice is part of all of life and history," says Dr. Stuart E. Rosenberg, Toronto (Canada) *Daily Star* columnist. This is especially true of Christianity, a religion that centers upon sacrifice and has its meaning in sacrifice.

Children are often reminded in Sunday-school literature that their bodies are the temples of the Holy Spirit[10] and that they ought to take care of them. Although this is true, we should not forget to tell our children that sacrifice of our bodies for Christ's sake is important also. Paul says: "Present your bodies a living sacrifice, holy, acceptable unto God, which is your reasonable service."[11] Permitting our bodies to be temples of the Holy Spirit and at the same time giving them as sacrifices to God are not opposing ideas. But the agreement is not in preservation of the body, but rather the burning of one's self out for a cause. Let us tell the pupils about Paul and his friend Epaphroditus who "for the work of Christ . . . was nigh unto death, not regarding his life."[12] Teach the children that Christianity all the way through is a religion of sacrifice. This lesson well learned is the heart of the practice of creative giving.

Let the children see the results of their giving. When a person knows what he is doing, how it helps, and whom it is for, he can more readily put his heart into his task of giving. If the pupils are to give to a missionary project, let them hear from the missionary in a letter. If they give to a local neighborhood house, let them take refreshments there and play games with the boys and girls in that house. Let them have a personal hand in giving. They will never become indifferent givers.

Let these additional maxims also govern the education of the child:

- Do not teach minimum or proportionate giving in any form.
- Play down athletics as a goal in itself; glorify lasting spiritual and

[10] 1 Corinthians 6: 19.
[11] Romans 12: 1.
[12] Philippians 2: 30.

sacrificial achievements—service vocations, and so on—rather than material and physical pursuits which are so infinitesimal compared to eternal values.

· Teach the whole Scripture, not prooftexts.

· Make the subject of "giving" the heart of the communicant, catechumenate, confirmation, or church membership class.

· "Saturate" pupils with content subjects of the Bible so that they will have a "well" from which to draw.

· Create opportunities of sharing to which pupils can respond.

· Separate the idea of regularity in giving from percentage or proportionate giving. (Proportion implies part of a whole—regularity implies a frequency. The two ideas are not necessarily mutually inclusive, as some assume. A person can give a proportion without being regular in his habits, and a person can give regularly without ever computing or setting aside a proportion.)

· Encourage imaginative, rather than literal, art styles in handwork activities.

· Do not be afraid of movies and other "live" visual aids to communicate the themes of giving.

· Apply a rigid but reasonable discipline at all times, for true creativity does not grow out of unbridled or unenlightened spontaneity.[13]

· Conduct a youth Every Member Canvass.

· Let the older youth have a hand in preparing the budget or their part of it.

· Arrange with the youth to meet with boards or agencies of the church, as the use and dispersion of money is discussed.

· Use creative lesson techniques such as role playing, socio-drama, pantomime.

· Plan special events, such as the White gift service, in which children can take part.

· Avoid a rigid observance of the Sabbath, permitting the youth to meet at a time other than the usual Sunday evening, if desired, such

[13] See Brewster Ghiselin, *The Creative Process* (Berkeley: University of California Press, 1952), p. 17.

as Tuesday night, as experimented with very successfully by a Waukegan (Illinois) American Baptist church.

· Encourage young people to take regular positions of service in the church, such as ushering, singing in the choir, calling.

· Emphasize missions and the calls of young people who gave all in order to serve Jesus. Enroll pupils in short-term mission projects and internships.

· Personal attention, such as visiting in the home or encouraging your pupils to send cards to the sick, can fan the spark within a child to personal faith in a personal redeemer.

· Avoid rote prayers—at church, at home, at the bedside, as they can pave the way of the child for static and rote giving.

· The spiritual rather than the showmanship side of prayer should be encouraged. (One mother learned this abruptly. She told her little boy who was saying his usual prayers at bedtime, "I can't hear you, Johnny!" to which the youngster answered, "I wasn't talking to you anyway!")

· Bring religion more into life by discussing such topics as smoking, obscene literature, petting, rather than the milktoast subjects such as carrying the Bible to Sunday school and sharing candy with a friend. Also related to this is an introduction of humor into teaching publications to show that religion is not a strait-jacket, but can be enjoyed as a spontaneous and real quality of life. An excellent example of this is the caricature art style used by the American Baptists in illustrating their senior-high evening-topic quarterly, *High Call.*

· Replace coloring books as far as possible with creative coloring and drawing. Color books and crutches go together, according to Dr. Viktor Lowenfeld, director of art education at Pennsylvania State University. "Once conditioned to coloring books, most children will have difficulties in enjoying freedom of creating," he says. "Research shows that more than half of all children, once exposed to coloring books, lose confidence in their creativeness, their independence of expression and become rigid."[14]

[14] *2-to-5 World News,* Feb., 1958.

· Encourage doubts to be brought out into the open and discussed, for "in dissipating every doubt, the human soul experiences one of the greatest joys of which it is capable."[15]

· Present Jesus as a living and abiding reality whom we can readily respond to and consult no matter where we may be.

In summary, if stewardship could give way to sacrifice, if anonymity in giving could be yielded in favor of personal relationships, if proportionate and rigid patterns of the church life could give way to an open, unrestricted sense of dedication, if both the issues and characteristics of life be recognized and discussed rather than the usual niceties on Sunday morning, the next generation of the church might be effectively creative in giving.

Change the seminary curriculum

To teach the church to be creative, first of all its leaders must be creative. Unfortunately, seminary training, although it is highly skilled, is not creative. It is primarily indoctrination which can be and often is anti-creative. When a minister can tell what seminary his fellow minister went to by the way he talks and thinks, then there was something drastically wrong with the seminary curriculum. I remember a student who, having just transferred from his own denominational seminary to a Presbyterian seminary, was elated to see one of his first test papers, on the philosophy of religion, come back with "A," and the comment, "At least you think!" which seems to have been a general indictment concerning the other papers submitted. He had been concerned about taking the risk of adjustment in an entirely new theological climate, but found that the change sharpened his intellect and presented a new challenge spiritually. The lesson in this for the denominations, and particularly for ecumenical Christianity, is to encourage a candidate for the ministry not to spend all of his three or four years in the denominational institution, where he will probably have reiterated what he believes

[15] Thomas V. Smith, *Creative Sceptics* (Chicago: Willett, Clark and Company, 1934), p. 248.

already, but to take at least one year in a different institution. One of the most creative and popular college professors I have known studied at the Roman Catholic Pontifical Institute of Medieval Studies in Toronto, Canada, not in preparing to become a priest, but in preparing to become a Baptist minister and teacher.

Concerning the curriculum in seminary, there are four general emphases which should stand out, as the church moves to train creative ministers:

1. In-service training programs such as preaching and pastoral experience on the field, counseling in detention homes and mental institutions, under the supervision of a field director. This approach is necessary if the church is to be relevant to its community. The next three emphases should be given more attention than they are now receiving.

2. As a doctor is no better than the basic instruments and skills of his profession, a minister cannot expect to be very efficient or creative without a thorough knowledge of the heart of the Bible itself, the Gospels of Jesus. And to understand them, he must know the language in which they are written, and do his own research. Otherwise he can do no more than mouth what someone else tells him, which is not a creative use of the Scriptures. As we have seen earlier in the discussion of tithing, for a minister to learn of the Gospels through secondary sources only can be dangerous for the church. *Proposal*: Three years of Greek for every seminary student, whether he passes it or not; two years of Hebrew, since the Old Testament is in Hebrew, and since Jesus, being a Jew, employed a number of Hebrew and Aramaic idioms. With this background, a minister can do his own thinking in the fundamentals of the faith. Less conformity and orthodoxy may be the result, but certainly there will also be more clarity of conviction and purpose.

3. Scrap the traditional approach to philosophy of religion. Instead of discussing what the philosophers of the past said about God as a *prima causa* and as transcendent or immanent, let the pupil study contemporary atheism, Communism, agnosticism, and positivism. In other words, let him face the hard knocks of contemporary

exist not for themselves but for witnessing for Christ, and that it is not a big achievement if they become self-supporting. . . . it is necessary to shift the emphasis from self-support to service for Christ."[16] Never present an end to giving. Giving goes beyond the local church, and there is no terminus to giving.

Place priority on Christian experience

There is still no substitute in the Christian faith for evangelism and the acceptance on the part of the individual of Christ as his own personal savior. "The marvelous generosity of the early Christians can be accounted for only by Christian experience."[17] Whatever the church can do from personal evangelism to mass evangelism will have a direct relationship in creative giving.

Do not underestimate the role of emotion in giving

In an effort to streamline giving procedures in the churches, the "old time" religion and the play on emotions have been widely discouraged as unhealthy. More emphasis is on rational approaches and on better business techniques. To put spontaneity into giving, emotion will have to be restored to giving. "Give me a church that has not lost all its means of spontaneous expression," says Daniel W. Boyer in "The Music of the Spiritual Church" in the Church of the Brethren's *Gospel Messenger,*[18] "a church that uses the dramatic; that renders me an occasional shock, a calculated shock. Obviously, I do not mean the shock from poor planning or no planning. Rather, the shock resulting from the emotionally expressed values from both the pulpit and choir loft." New Testament giving was emotionally charged; and giving that is to achieve a degree of the spontaneity of the early church will be emotional giving.

[16] V. S. Azariah, *Christian Giving* (London: Lutterworth Press, 1954), pp. 42, 43.

[17] Henry Burton Trimble, *The Christian Motive and Method in Stewardship* (Nashville: Abingdon Press, 1929), p. 157.

[18] Aug. 17, 1957 issue, p. 11.

anti-Christian thinking. This is what Chicago's McCormick (Pres
terian) Seminary is doing when in its required philosophy-of
ligion course it begins mildly with such men as Ralph Wa
Emerson, William James, and John Dewey in the first semester a
ends the second with the positivistic Alfred Jules Ayer, existential
Jean-Paul Sartre, and several thinkers barely inside traditional Chr
tianity, Russian Orthodox Nicolas Berdyaev and Roman Cathol
Gabriel Marcel. Subjects for term papers are not St. Augustin
Calvin, and Jonathan Edwards, but rather non-christian philosopher
novelists, and political figures such as Earl Browder, former secre
tary of the Communist party. Special courses are also offered in
readings in German from the atheistic existentialist Martin
Heidegger, and in French of Jean-Paul Sartre's basic works. This does
not exclude research in Augustine, Luther, and Calvin which helps
students to face the problems of contemporary society. But with
exposure to contemporary religion in its various forms the minister-to-be is at home in any college or industrial bull session, and not
just at home in his own tower.

4. Ministers need to have a clear distinction between material and spiritual values, between extrinsic and intrinsic values. Ministers, as well as other church people, occasionally reflect confusion in the very basics of the faith, such as what has the most value, as is indicated in some of the things they say and in the way they spend their money. They are human too. But perhaps all Christians should consider what the greatest values are and which are eternal. Ministers should be the first to know the differences and where the emphases should be. Value should be taught as activity, as something personal, as that which is felt, and not only as abstraction or only as that which is concrete or seen. *Proposal*: A required course in the philosophy of value for every minister.

Present an unlimited demand

The late Bishop Azariah of India, quoting a survey of an Indian city and its churches, said: "The churches need to realize that they

Relate church architecture to giving

"A well designed church fairly shouts the beliefs of those who worship there," says Edward S. Frey, executive director of the department of architecture for the United Lutheran Church in America. "Every part of the building—the windows, the chancel, the furnishings, even the floor plan—is vocal."[19] As the church encourages creative faith and giving among its members, there should be a symbolism, such as the cross, to illustrate God's giving and to encourage man's giving; the floor plan should allow ample space for freedom of activity and expression; the colors can be chosen for the atmosphere that is to be created and for their symbolism. For example: "Red doors, which happily are becoming more common, speak of Christian zeal and tell that through the shedding of Christ's blood we enter into eternal life with him."

Let there be a single focal point in the sanctuary which calls for response and commitment. A Chicago Baptist church has Lorado Taft's famous bas-relief "Come unto Me" at the focal point of attention; Lutheran and Episcopal churches have the altar.

Pastor Herbert Reich of the Evangelical Lutheran Church in Hanover, Germany, tells about a visitor who came into a church as the workers were putting the final touches on the sanctuary. They were painting the last wall. At first the visitor was pleased with what he saw, but when he caught sight of the long wall above the altar, where a picture of the Good Shepherd was being painted, all he could see was a few firm strokes, outlining the head and shoulders of Christ. Part of a staff was indicated, but nothing more.

The visitor turned to a workman. "That picture. When will it be finished?"

"That picture," said the workman, "*is* finished."

"What do you mean, 'finished'? Most of it is still missing—the hands, feet, mouth, arms, legs—in fact, the whole body is gone!"

[19] "What Do Church Buildings Say?" *New Christian Advocate,* Sept., 1957, p. 22.

"You won't see that on the wall," the workman said. "The body of Christ is the congregation of people who will be worshiping here in this church. The body of Christ is the church!"

All church designs—contemporary or otherwise—that carry a similar meaning directly through their symbols spur creative participation and giving.

Avoid unchristian ways of giving

"The first thing to do is to abandon all unchristian ways, now in vogue, of raising money for God's work. By this we mean not only the giving up of all lotteries, raffles, and all other methods intended merely to make people give in exchange for a little excitement or enjoyment. We mean also the methods of assessment: church-tax and compulsory fees for the administration of sacraments now prevailing in many churches. Along with these must also go all penal methods of enforcing the payment of church dues. Giving must be lifted up to the level of spontaneity and voluntariness, and set free from all ideas of compulsion by threat of public exposure or open disgrace, or by exclusion from privileges."[20] This would include the recognition of gifts from the pulpit or by published "honor rolls," and the sanction and merit associated with the tithe.

Eliminating unchristian ways of giving might affect the use of statistics to the point of de-emphasizing them, if not to the point of banning statistics altogether. It might affect the relating of our church giving with income-tax deductions. One church paper said recently: "Of every tax dollar you pledge, if you have any taxable income, the Government is going to be paying 20 to 50 cents or more." Any cause worth giving to, including the Federal government, is worth giving to directly. The above quotation is from a Baptist paper which vociferously deplores church-state tie-ins in some areas, but not in regard to giving. Certainly giving that is to be effective and creative and sincere need not base its appeal on kickbacks from a Federal tax. We would object to a procedure of taxation that

[20] Azariah, *op. cit.*, p. 86.

gives special disposition to the party-loyal in a Communist country. Americans ought to protest the same arrangement in a free country.

Delete non-Christian ideas in promotion of giving

The endorsement of tithing by the major denominational bodies in the United States encourages some wild statements. For example, such ideas as "A series of surprises await the tither" and "There is magic in tithing" can be found in promotion literature. All unholy promotion should be corrected; the spiritual emphases can stand alone without the aid of questionable secular devices. The use of prooftexts, especially out of context, should be deleted from promotion copy. "There is the ill-directed use of Malachi 3: 10, which often misleads people to think of giving to God as a bargain with God. We do not give because we want to receive; we give because we have received."[21] Keep the sales-pitch of the church straight. Wonders will be worked in regard to the influence of the church in the community. "There can be little doubt that the low esteem in which the church is held in some communities is a result of the cheap and tawdry—the irreverent—methods it has used on many occasions for raising funds with which to carry on God's work."[22]

Present "not-giving" as a state of sin

Protestants could take a cue from Roman Catholics who label certain actions as sin, thus encouraging specific attitudes of living. A key to writing fiction is to select a villain. Against the villain the protagonist or hero struggles and emerges. If the opposite of giving, a theoretical state of "not-giving," were to be labeled as "sin" or "villain," giving would take a new prominence in Christian theology. At the next gathering of professors and theologians of the denomination or at the next area stewardship meeting, how about drafting a

[21] *Ibid.*, p. 87.

[22] Roy L. Smith, *Stewardship Studies* (New York: Abingdon Press, 1954), p. 58.

statement like this one formulated by the Catholic Synod of Baltimore in 1791? It said: . . . "When in proportion to the world goods with which God has endowed them, they [parishioners] refuse to contribute to the ministry of salvation, and so do not satisfy the Divine and ecclesiastical precept through their own fault, let them know they are in a state of sin and unworthy of obtaining reconciliation in the tribunal of penance; and moreover that they will have to give an account to God, not only for their own sin, but also for the dense ignorance and vices of the poor who on account of the miserable parsimony of the richer people are entirely deprived of Christian instruction."[23]

Let Protestant ministers not only talk about giving; let them also put steel into this privilege and opportunity which is at the heart of their faith. For what greater sin can there be in the world than for a man through pride and selfishness to fail to give his heart and life to Jesus Christ, or for Christians to fail to live in a giving relationship with Christ their redeemer and with their fellow men? Let us speak of "not-giving" as sin, and a cardinal sin at that.

There is much that Western Christianity, having become dull in its influence in the world, and in its own back yard, can do to be creative. Concentrating on even a few of the areas mentioned above can do wonders concerning the church's creative influence on society and on international tensions. But the real crux is not so much what the church should do as that it should move in the direction of creativity and really *want* to be creative. That is what counts. A repentant, confessing church that is right with its Lord and that is consistent with the working of the Holy Spirit will be creative, in spite of human weaknesses. Precisely how it can become creative, of course, must always rest ultimately with the Spirit of God.

[23] William H. W. Fanning, "Church Maintenance," *The Catholic Encyclopedia* (New York: The Encyclopedia Press, Inc., 1913), III, 763.

5

How to Give Creatively

To encourage creative giving, the man who gives must not be overlooked. And he wants to know *how* to give creatively. We need a formula for giving. That is why proportionate giving has been so popular—it has a clear, concise, workable formula.

Creative giving can be diagrammed in relationship to proportionate giving. By comparing the two different ways of giving at the same points, we see not only where proportionate giving takes us, but also where creative giving will take us in terms of practice. Perhaps this attempt at simplification is over-exaggerated, but by attempting to draw a line between two opposing views and by comparing them at specific points exaggeration makes explicit the differences. Even as exaggeration and caricature have the function of clarification and of approaching reality in art, so can simplification clarify the differences between two points of view.

It is granted that the parties who promote each of these two types of giving or who try to promote both would sincerely like to see the revitalization of the church. But the means to the same proposed end are not the same. Now consider these points of comparison:

	Proportionate Giving	Creative Giving
Starting point	A principle (divine ownership, etc.)	A person (Jesus Christ)
Sanctions found in	Status quo	Individual
Subject	Man (recognizing his weakness)	Man (recognizing his redemption)
Type of action encouraged	Habit	Spontaneity
Frequency of action	Regularity	Irregularity and/or regularity
Relationships	Impersonal	Personal
Quantity	A percentage (with a given minimum)	Totality
Appeal based on	Prooftexts	The whole Bible
Motives	1. To finance the church 2. To grow in the faith 3. To say "thank you" to God	None (Giving is out of a response. The nearest thing to a motive is the childlike answer "Because," "Because Christ came.")

Proportionate giving calls for definite steps and right actions to be taken. The formula goes like this: Give a proportion back to God—a proportion of money, time—with one-tenth of a person's income and one-seventh of his time as starting points for all Christians. Creative giving, with the emphasis on total commitment and freedom and personality in giving, is not concerned with the right actions or sanctions of a principle. The formula for creative giving can only be in terms of non-directive procedures, such as asking questions.

Now if we had clung literally to the ideal in Christian giving, spontaneity, and refused to recognize man as a sinner, then we could never ask a question. For to pause to ask a question or to reflect on something is to deviate from spontaneity, even though our pause be only for a moment. But we have decided to look for spontaneity in life and to look for that giving which is the closest to spontaneity and which is at the same time practical. This we can do, and at the same time we shall ask creative questions.

I

The starting point in creative giving is in asking questions, and primarily one question: "How can I give everything?"

Our question is not like the proportionate giver's question, "How *much* shall I give?" We refrain from placing the question in any category except that realm of totality which encompasses all categories. Totality is not quantity; quantity implies parts or sums of parts; "all" supersedes quantity and makes quantitative distinctions unnecessary. The creative question is simply "how"—"how can I give *everything*?" leaving the definition of it to the working of the Spirit within.

By giving everything we do not mean annihilation or the giving up of everything one has and becoming a monk or hermit. That is contrary to life. It is slavery to a principle and is anti-personal, anti-Christian. Creative giving is not segregated from the community or from other persons. Giving in its highest and most creative sense is not asceticism, but utility. Therefore we can restate the basic question of our formula in this manner: "How can I *use* everything for God?"

How can I give, or use, everything?

First, invoking the work of the Holy Spirit in guiding us, let us begin with the tangible things of life.

Begin by listing everything you own. Everything. For example, the car, house, sewing machine, refrigerator, golf clubs, clothes, books, magazines, scissors, pencils, powder puff, electric razor, snow shovel, lawn mower, toothbrush, Pinky the rabbit, hammer, saw, and so on, and of course the billfold and the cash in it, or that which is represented by it.

Encourage the children and other members of the family to list what they own, too, for example, the color books, paste, crayons, dolls, deer rifle, formal clothes.

What a silly way to begin to think about giving! Let us go on. What do we do next?

Now ask, "How can I give or use this or that item for Christ?"

Put an answer after every item. If it cannot be used, perhaps it ought to be discarded or replaced.

It will be seen that the sewing machine can be used to make garments for an orphanage or choir robes for acolytes; the snow shovel or lawn mower might be used to help a neighbor or shut-in; the stove, sink, refrigerator, and other kitchen utensils can be used to prepare meals for a family night at church, a youth supper, a sick neighbor or church member. A child can take a plain piece of paper and crayons and create his own get-well card for Grandpa, or he can model a dish of clay for a friend.

Alongside the car, put down ways it can be used for God's work, such as making church calls, transporting older people on Sunday morning, driving to and taking part in a pioneer project of organizing a new church outside the community, regular trips for Sunday school. If a person sees no possible use of such an item as a car for his church or similar Kingdom work, he seriously ought to think whether he should have bought the car.

What kind of hobbies do we have? Gardening, of course, can provide flowers and food for certain occasions of the church or for others; music can be shared. Handwork also has utility. For example, the late James L. Kraft, founder of the Kraft Foods Company, ground precious stones and jade late every night at his work bench in his basement—and gave away all the results of his labors at church or as service awards in his business. There are many, many other creative hobbies, such as writing to pen pals and to the sick. Building, designing, painting, and drawing demand creative expression and have creative uses at church. But not all hobbies are creative as far as utility is concerned. Consider the "hobbies of hoarding"—for instance, stamp collecting, coin or match-cover collecting. These are generally self-centered. However, the emphasis could be shifted more to collecting and giving than to hoarding. When a movie star was asked recently why he was giving away and selling his collection of art treasures, which included works of Picasso and other famous artists, he answered simply that the fun was in the collecting and not in the keeping. Have a creative hobby that permits not only creative expression, but also creative giving.

When buying or building a house, a couple ought to ask, "How can we give our house?" If they truly wish to include their house in giving, they might want to include one more bedroom in their plans, with the view of caring for a guest—a refugee, an older person, a child or adult recommended for home care by the courts or a social or religious organization. One Chicago lady and her husband, although they had two healthy children of their own, adopted a so-called handicapped child and in a period of years brought him up to be a healthy youngster, a good student and athlete. There can be creative giving in regard to parenthood.

Several years ago I met Abbé Pierre, the rag-picking priest of Paris, who had just come to the United States. "What is needed the most, and is lacking now," he said, "is a personal touch." It was his thesis that the multitudes of needy and spiritually sick about us should be "grafted into families."

This is a very strange thought indeed for the average Western Christian who holds his family hearth the most sacred of all, the holy of holies. To bring a total stranger into his home would be to profane it. But Abbé Pierre had an intelligent solution, for to bring the really needy into the most personal and sacred of our experiences is to extend a healing hand to unfortunate members of an impersonal society whom it is difficult to assist or affect in any other way.

Consider the significance of entertaining strangers in the account of Abraham entertaining the three strangers and in the New Testament account of the two men on the road to Emmaus entertaining the stranger that approached them. Abraham entertained three angels; the disciples on the road entertained in their home the risen Jesus. When we sing "We Would See Jesus," we ought to be careful to see that we are not closing the door of our own home to him.

Under the Refugee Relief Act of 1953, the Methodist Committee on Overseas Relief made a special effort to sponsor in Christian homes Moslems and other non-Christians. Most of these people, especially the Moslems, are very difficult to reach on the mission field. Introducing and leading people to Christ by opening the home can become an effective tool of evangelism. Christian deeds can go further than words in today's battle of ideologies.

When a 16-year-old Olympic medal winner, Nancy Ramey of Seattle, Washington, prepared to go home after the games in Melbourne in 1956, she made plans with her parents to take with her Hungarian refugee Zsusza "Susie" Ordogh. The fact that Susie was Roman Catholic and could not speak English did not stop Lutheran Nancy. Having Susie come to America to stay with her was one of the greatest experiences she has ever had, Nancy explains. It is Nancy's belief that the spirit of good will at the Olympics can be repeated in local communities around the world. The tall, enthusiastic blond who breaks records nearly every time she swims (among her latest: the AAU and American record in the breast stroke in April, 1958) has hopes of becoming a missionary. This shows today's adults that eliminating the usual provincialism and self-containment in giving, even to the point of opening the home as the Ramey family did, can leave striking religious marks on the youth of the household.

The home can be used for prayer meetings, Bible study, cell groups, youth meetings and church social activities. International students can be entertained on such holidays as Thanksgiving, Christmas, and Easter.

A couple might want to include a symbol of giving in the interior decorating of their home to remind them of the place of giving in the Christian faith. Some homes, particularly more well-to-do homes, have a display of plants or another attraction in the foyer of the house, sometimes with a lighting effect. In place of such an arrangement, why could not a home in which a perpetual consciousness of giving is encouraged have a wrought-iron cross set aside near the door with indirect lighting casting a shadow of the cross across the threshold? Concerning the type of house a Christian has, the kind of house is not so important as how he uses it, although we shall see that something can be said for economy in living. When approaching creatively the subject of using the house, it would seem that a person ought to live near those in need or, if he prefers suburban comfort, to take those in need to him. Creative giving in practice is not a life of separation.

If a man really has a personal concern for his neighbor, and is willing to inject the idea of personality into his real-estate investments, creative giving can enter the problem of real estate and the race question. When a member of a different race moves into an all-white area causing real estate values to fall drastically, Christians sometimes become angry because they cannot see beyond property values and the dollar sign. However, if Christians can be made to realize that there is such a thing as personality investment along with property investment, they could strike off some of their financial setback as personality investment.

How about money? After all, it is money that pays the day-by-day bills of the church. According to the "Didache," or "teaching" of the twelve apostles, some of the early Christians were to give "firstfruits to the prophets."[1] This is an intelligent way to give, though not without consideration of a person's own family obligations and his other investments. For example, one man let his gifts for the church accumulate over a seven-year period in a bank with a good interest rate, then turned the money and interest over to the church. This is of course not always practical where bills must be met. But it does show that giving is not merely an unenlightened division of the pay check. All things considered, a person should place his giving to the church as high as possible, pay this bill first, ahead of his other commitments, so that he will not be tempted to scrimp his church giving. Giving to the church should be done with regularity, as often as one receives a pay check. But giving the "firstfruits" and giving "regularly" are not the same as giving a predetermined proportion. If tithing could be made to mean only "firstfruits" and "regularity," if it could be separated from its fictional and historical background, and if it could be disregarded as a starting point, then tithing would be an acceptable term in

[1] James A. Kleist, *Ancient Christian Writers,* "The Didache" (Westminster, Md.: The Newman Press, 1948), p. 23.

giving. But unfortunately tithing means basically and literally a "tenth," which disqualifies it as a useful word in giving, when a total, creative approach is made to the dispersal of money for the Kingdom of God.

We have covered the range of a man's physical possessions. Glancing over the list of all our possessions, it is absurd to say that we can give and use everything on that list to the furtherance of the Kingdom. There are always such items as the toothbrush, the electric razor, the powder puff. But even these items can have a Christian utility. If we use them to make us clean and presentable to others, we show that we personally care about those we meet in the world, not wishing to offend them. In so doing, we prepare the way for a creative giving or presentation of our personalities and that for which we stand. When our possessions fail to make us presentable, and carry us to the point of overdressing and painted absurdity, they ought to be discarded.

A sense of dedication and utility should pervade the use of everything we have. Roman Catholics have carried this to the point of blessing objects, such as a house, a crop, ocean vessels, iron furnaces, cars about to be taken on a trip, and so on. When fees are collected, this procedure brings problems that are not too different from those resulting from the fees and indulgences collected in the Middle Ages. At least the idea of dedication is good for Protestants as long as it remains with the individual and not in the hands of a clergyman. For since no thought is foreign to God, and no object is beyond God, nothing should be used without first invoking His benediction on it and on the application of the object or desire in His use. Paul sums up the idea: "And whatsoever ye do in word or deed, do all in the name of the Lord Jesus."[2] Again he says: "Whether therefore ye eat, or drink, or whatsoever ye do, do all to the glory of God."[3] A Christian's giving is summed up in his using of his whole life and acquisitions for the Kingdom of God.

We have applied the "question of giving" to the area of the

[2] Colossians 3: 17.
[3] 1 Corinthians 10: 31.

things we see and touch. How about the things that are not seen, the things that are intangible? Creative giving seeks them out, too, as it includes everything in the experience of the Christian.

If proportionate giving speaks of giving a seventh of a person's time to the church, what then will creative giving speak of in regard to time?

Let us begin again with the total idea, that is, "How can we give everything?"

Let us approach our answer analytically again. What does a person's time consist of?

Basically a man's conscious hours fall into two categories—work and leisure, the job and recreation, or more generally, vocation and vacation.

How can a person give on his job?

That depends, of course, on what his job is, but there are some basic suggestions for giving on a job that apply to most circumstances. Among them are:

1. *A person should give his best energy and thought to his job.* Working hard trains a man for other direct ways of giving—the busy man always has time for something else. Because a person's monetary productivity will be related to his work and ambition, giving his best to his job means giving his best to his church, which makes demands on his time and income.

2. *Do the unpleasant task first.* A person can make the most undesirable job the most attractive and important if he approaches it in a Christian spirit. Christ's approach to the cross was hard, and thrice he asked that the cup might pass from him, but he did the will of his Father. Performing a secular job also has meaning, for in it we fulfill our main responsibility on earth. Accept the unattractive, insignificant job and do it well. To do so will revitalize all persons involved, including yourself.

3. *Give something of the faith.* By what a person says, as well as by the way he acts at his place of work, he can be a witness for Christ. If Christ abides in a person, the person's friends will know it. They may inquire about the Christian's faith, or the Christian may interpolate an explanation of his faith in his reasoning for doing a certain thing. Since a person spends the larger part of his creative and active hours at work, Jesus' Great Commission would be very effective there: "Go ye into all the world, teaching all nations"—or all employees. The Christian has much to give at work.

Giving at work does not always need to be directly evangelical. "The kind of giving I would emphasize," says Philip R. Clarke, former Chicago banker and now chairman of the executive committee of Montgomery Ward, "is the everyday pattern that is within the power of each of us—such as giving consideration to the other fellow and his viewpoint—giving courtesy instead of a snub or indifference—giving sympathetic attention to a friend who has a problem, and above all else, giving complete integrity to one's daily task. By that I mean giving one's honest, conscientious best to one's job, whatever it may be. Because the satisfying sense of accomplishment that one gets back from such giving—from a job well done—is one of the most gratifying forces of all, in carrying on a successful life."

Mr. Clarke adds: "Finally, every one of us can and must give our loyalty to those causes which stand for lawful freedom of the individual and against enslavement of his mind and spirit." There are many ideas with which a Christian can align himself at work—for example, (1) that which is fair to all, including competitors; (2) that which builds personality instead of that which denigrates personality, such as the off-color joke; (3) that which recognizes responsible use of money, not such practices as lotteries, betting, World Series pools, and other careless uses of money at work.

How can a person give his leisure time?

If he has hobbies, we have seen ways in which creative giving can enter. Even on vacations giving need not be excluded. For example, if a minister or layman is going on a prayer retreat and can afford travel expenses, he ought to see to it that someone, lay or clergy, who might not be able to, but who would like to participate in the same endeavor, should be enabled to do so. If a person is planning a trip for the sake of his health, perhaps he ought to inquire if there is someone nearby who might benefit similarly on the same trip. A person going on a vacation can take along a lonely adult, a handicapped person, or a child from an underprivileged home or from an institution.

In endeavoring to put leisure time to use, a retired Chicago advertising salesman, Frank W. Quayle, and his wife, found the owner of a nearby lot and persuaded him to permit the property to be used as a playground. The Quayles paid for the equipment. From morning to sunset each day this elderly couple supervised the playground activities. Eventually the Quayles talked the city authorities into purchasing the lot for a permanent playground. The Quayles did not stop with this activity. Each year for sixteen years they took more than one hundred children to the Shrine circus. Even after the boys and girls grew up, whenever they saw the Quayles on the street they would run up to them and say, "Remember me? I used to play in your lot and go to the circus with you." The leisure time of old age can be given or used creatively too.

Creative giving in practice is very simple. It is no more than asking the general question "How can I give everything I have?" which when made specific to each item of life elicits creative giving. The question itself is not synonymous with spontaneity, but by involving the whole personality and by stirring the depths of a committed life the creative giving that results comes closer to ideal spontaneity than any other type of giving.

II

No rules are needed in creative giving, but there is one that will help. For when it is considered that creativity involves the whole man, any rule which gears man to respond at his fullest capacity will be conducive to creativity. Such a rule for creative giving is found in economizing, conserving, restricting the efforts of the individual. "All creativity—in art, in music, in architecture, in literature—involves *economizing*—that is, making the most of a set of limitations. . . . It is *because* the artist is limited by his material that art exists." Where there is "no scarcity, no limitation—there is no art, only formless and cancerous growth."[4]

When the creative giver, as well as the artist, is limited he can give more creatively. Again we would not confuse this idea of limitation with quantity, for we are not to suggest in terms of amount how much a person should be limited, but simply that he should economize and conserve in order that he may use.

This leads us to suggest a rule for creative giving: Be stingy. And not irreverently we say, "Be stingy for Christ's sake." We should be stingy to the utmost as we live the Christian faith. We are not talking of being a miser, where one hoards up all one can for oneself. Being stingy for Christ's sake places a limitation only in the light of a total commitment, when one's whole life is in the hands of an active, participating Christ.

This rule of being stingy puts a bite into Christianity. All our axons feel the pang of it, as surely as the body of Christ was racked with the blows upon the nails being driven into his flesh. Giving in the light of the cross is not a pleasant thought for a worldly creature. Only a fool, such as a miser, or a religious man, such as a Christian, can live in a practice of stinginess. Being stingy for Christ's sake is a privilege and an opportunity for a Christian in regard to his creative role in life.

Here is how practicing restraint in living may be accomplished.

Money. One summer while studying at the Medill School of Journalism, Northwestern University, I had the privilege of staying in the home of Mr. and Mrs. James L. Kraft. Mr. Kraft was a Baptist layman, and chairman of the board of the Kraft Foods Company. There were many examples of sacrificial giving on their part; yet

[4] Kenneth E. Boulding, professor of economics, University of Michigan, from "Some Contributions of Economics to Theology and Religion," *Religious Education,* Nov.-Dec., 1957, p. 450.

one occasion in the following summer stands out as a clue to their striking philosophy of giving. The Krafts were taking me home to the rooming house in which I was staying. Mrs. Kraft suggested that we stop for some refreshment, knowing that a college student always enjoys a soda or milkshake. As we were leaving the drugstore Mrs. Kraft in paying the bill questioned the cashier concerning the charge of a few extra cents. This might seem strange, but Mrs. Kraft a short time before had just given her only valuable piece of jewelry, a diamond bracelet (a special keepsake from her husband), to the foreign mission work of the American Baptists. The value of this keepsake was $15,000. She was indeed concerned "for Christ's sake." Important areas of Christendom flourished because of the giving of herself and of her husband. One of these areas was a mission station in India supported completely at their own expense.

For Christians to face Communism effectively and creatively, minimum living with restraint in spending will have to influence their giving. A French Communist party newspaper in France recently said: "Of our salaries and wages we keep only what is strictly necessary and we give up the rest for propaganda purposes. To this propaganda we also consecrate all our free time and part of our holidays." This statement is much different from one recently appearing in a Christian evangelical publication which said quite directly that God expects the Christian to move from one level of comfort to another. Creative Christian giving, however, calls for recognizing a commitment, and for living at a minimum so that one can give a maximum.

The creative giver can take his cue from John Wesley in regard to a philosophy of money. "Having *gained,* in a right sense, *all you can,* and *saved all you can:* in spite of nature, and custom, and world prudence, *give all you can.*"[5] For John Wesley, giving a tenth, or giving a half as Zacchaeus did, was fine and should be commended. But he follows with the exciting suggestion: "But yet I show unto you 'a more excellent' way." He tells of the practice of the young men at Oxford. One (presumably himself) received

[5] From "The Danger of Riches," *Arminian Magazine,* 1781.

thirty pounds in his first year and found that his maintenance required twenty-eight. The young man gave away the surplus of two pounds. "The next year, receiving sixty pounds, he still lived on twenty-eight, and gave away two and thirty. The third year he received ninety pounds, and gave away sixty-two. The fourth year he received a hundred and twenty pounds. Still he lived as before on twenty-eight; and gave to the poor ninety-two. Was not this a more excellent way?"[6] Strive to keep expenses at a minimum—a minimum which, unlike Wesley's case, is bound to change with a rise in the cost of living; then give the rest away, as Wesley recommends. See in your own heart if this total approach, with parsimony, is not a more excellent way than giving proportionately.

Traveling. When Albert Schweitzer arrived in his native Alsace, in France, for a visit in September, 1957, a group of students and reporters met him at the train. Schweitzer had traveled as cheaply as he could. "Why did you travel second class?" one of the crowd asked. "Because," said Schweitzer, "there was no third class." When time permits, business executives and others might use less expensive surface transportation instead of flying.

House. When a couple finishes purchasing a house and begins to accumulate savings, what is the next step? Should it be a bigger and better house? Should the move be from an old frame house in an older part of town to a ranch-style model in the countryside? If a person is stingy for Christ's sake, what should his decision be? The decision, of course, is a personal one, and it is not the purpose of this book to be arbitrary in matters of giving and investments. However, we might suggest an alternative in the light of our rule for giving: give the house away, to the church to sell or to the church to lease to an old couple or needy family, and then buy another house in the same bracket, instead of moving to the dream house. After all, life is too short to seek heaven on earth—there is all eternity for a Christian to enjoy heaven.

Wesley suggests restraint in decorating one's house. "Do not

[6] From "The More Excellent Way," *Arminian Magazine,* 1787.

waste any part of so precious a talent (money or ability) merely in gratifying the desire of the eye. . . . Waste no part of it in curiously adorning your houses; in superfluous or expensive furniture; in costly pictures, painting, gilding, books; in elegant rather than useful gardens. Let your neighbours, who know nothing better, do this: 'let the dead bury their dead.' "[7]

Farming. Three-fourths of the land in the United States which can be cultivated is subject to erosion. The Christian who farms can conserve land not only for his own sake but for the sake of those who will be using it after he is gone from the scene. By being thrifty and careful with his land, he can leave a legacy for many generations to enjoy.

Using the spare moment. C. H. Allen in the unpublished English translation of his *Christian Stewardship,* the Persian version of which was published in connection with his work as a Presbyterian (U.S.A.) missionary in Iran, pleads for parsimony in regard to time. "In every day we have spare moments, fragments of time between this and that. Lunch is not ready right on time, or a caller comes late and you have to wait for him. What do you do with these bits of time? Most people waste them. They pick up a newspaper, or engage in idle talk, or just sit around doing nothing. . . . It is a great thing to be able to use these fragments of time wisely." He points out that if the average person would add up all of these spare moments, he would see that he is wasting four or five years in a lifetime. The creative giver makes use of every moment: if he is on a subway he reads, or practices memorization, such as Scripture or vocabulary lists; at home he indulges in his hobby, organizes his work, plays with his children, reads, or even rests, which is more creative than looking at the "funnies" or watching the end of a TV movie.

Eating. "Stinginess for Christ's sake" can be applied three times a day in the way a person eats. Internationally famous violinist octo-

[7] From the sermon, "The Use of Money."

genarian Fritz Kreisler explains that he constantly tries to keep his needs to a minimum. "I feel morally guilty when I order a costly meal," he says, "for it might deprive someone else of a slice of bread —some child, perhaps, of a bottle of milk." The average worker who has an opportunity to buy a lunch daily can apply this same idea by bringing a prepared lunch from his home, thus cutting his daily expense and releasing more funds for his church. The same philosophy can be instilled into our children. For example, students at the Masters School, Dobbs Ferry, New York, eat a "slim lunch" on Thursdays. In one year the difference saved between the cost of the regular lunch and a "slim lunch" came to $911. This money is given to charities.

The use of leftovers in preparing new dishes can give place to novelty, which is a basic denominator of all creativity, just as economizing is a basis to creativity. Among the Lutheran churches of Assam and South India, there is the beautiful practice of Chatu Sirni, as it is called in Assam. The housewife, as she prepares to put the rice into the boiling caldron, takes out a handful of rice and puts it by, to be given to the church. The American housewife, who does not boil rice every day, could follow the Indian woman's example and take a few coins from her daily budget, instead of rice, to use in some way for the cause of Christ and his church.

Appearance. Seventh-day Adventists, who always head the list in per capita giving, apply the idea of minimum living not only to food but also to appearance, which is also an emphasis of small fundamental groups springing from Wesleyan, Puritan, and pietistic traditions. Seventh-day Adventists "believe that they should not knowingly wear anything, or use anything, to attract attention to themselves. Their sole desire is to attract attention to their Lord. They find in the Bible explicit injunctions against dressing lavishly and extravagantly, against the use of gold and precious stones, and other trinkets for the purpose of adornment."[8] Realizing that the

[8] Carlyle B. Haynes, *Seventh-day Adventists* (Washington: Review and Herald Publishing Association, 1940), p. 79.

most real things are those not seen, Adventists prefer to concentrate on a sense of destiny, a second coming of Christ, rather than on personal adornment. This sense of destiny no doubt explains to a great extent the volume of their giving, which in addition to their legalistic giving of 10 per cent and freewill offerings was to include a $1,000,000 campaign for missions in June of 1958.

Being stingy—living at a minimum—and literally giving all are ideas that take on meaning in the light of destiny. A Christian is a creature of the future as well as of the present. What he gives and how he gives have eternal significance.

Eusebius, Constantine's biographer, records a conversation between the great emperor and one of his attendants. "'How far, my friend,' said Constantine, 'are we to carry our inordinate desires?' Then drawing the dimensions of a human figure with a lance which he happened to have in his hand, he continued: 'Though thou couldst obtain the whole wealth of this world, yea, the whole world itself, thou wilt carry with thee at last no more than this little spot which I have marked out; if indeed even that be thine.'"[9] Although man is an owner, he leaves this world completely destitute as far as worldly things are concerned. "For we brought nothing into this world," says Paul, "and it is certain we can carry nothing out."[10] The Christ on the cross was out of place in this life and so are those who take up that cross. Yet the way of the cross and of sacrifice is the way of meaningful religion. "The path which man has to tread in this life lies through suffering, the cross and death, but it leads on towards resurrection."[11] It is this resurrection—the presence of a creative destiny—that the Christian recognizes in his newness of life. He lives for each moment to be a breakthrough of the Spirit. The Christian's course is not one of deliberation, but of response.

[9] Eusebius, "The Life of Constantine," from *A Select Library of Nicene and Post-Nicene Fathers of the Christian Church,* Philip Schaff and Henry Wace, editors (New York: Parker and Company, 1890), I, 548.

[10] 1 Timothy 6: 7.

[11] Berdyaev, *Slavery and Freedom,* p. 267.

Each moment of a Christian's day constitutes a potential point of activity for the Spirit of God. "I am the vine, ye are the branches: He that abideth in me, and I in him, the same bringeth forth much fruit: for without me ye can do nothing."[12]

Creative giving involves sacrifice, a person's total endeavor, his personal attention, his constant, spontaneous decision.

"Whosoever will come after me, let him deny himself, and take up his cross, and follow me."[13] Giving, according to Jesus, takes the symbol of the cross, and giving that is creative is best described in terms of spontaneity in the light of destiny. For "whosoever shall lose his life for my sake," says Jesus, "the same shall save it."

[12] John 15: 5.
[13] Mark 8: 34.

General Index

Scripture Index